GLOBAL CHANGER

STUDENT'S BOOK AND WORKBOOK

1

VIVIANE KIRMELIENE, DENISE SANTOS,
LIZ WALTER AND KATE WOODFORD WITH PAULO MACHADO

CAMBRIDGE
UNIVERSITY PRESS

CONTENTS

* This material can be downloaded from the Digital Resource Pack.

WELCOME!

FAMILY

1 0.01 **Complete the family tree with the words below. Then listen, check, and repeat.**

- aunt
- brother
- cousin
- dad
- ~~grandma~~
- grandpa
- mom
- sister
- uncle

POSSESSIVE ADJECTIVES

2 Complete the chart with the correct words.

		Possessive Adjectives
Singular	I	my
	you	1 your
	he	2 ______
	she	3 ______
	it	its
Plural	we	4 ______
	you	5 ______
	they	6 ______

3 Use possessive adjectives to complete the sentences.

1 My friend Zoë and I do ...our... homework at school.
2 Hi, ______ name's James. What's your name?
3 Emma loves ______ new bike. She takes it everywhere.
4 You have a lot of clothes. Is ______ closet big?
5 This is the new student. ______ name is Pedro.
6 My sisters like sports. ______ favorite class is PE.

POSSESSIVE ('S)

4 Rewrite the sentences so that they have the same meaning. Use the possessive ('s).

1 Dan has brown hair.
Dan's hair is brown.
2 Maria has blue eyes.
______
3 My mom has long hair.
______
4 My cousin has a big yard.
______

USE IT!

5 Draw your family tree. Ask and answer questions with a partner.

Who's that?

That's my uncle. His name's Mario.

VERB *TO BE*

1 0.02 **Complete the labels with the countries (C) and nationalities (N). Then listen, check, and repeat the words and letters.**

1

C: Brazil
N: Brazil i a n

2

C: The Uni_ _ _ States
N: _ _ _ _ _ can

3

C: Japan
N: Japan_ _ _

2 0.03 **Complete the post with *'m*, *'m not*, *is*, or *are*. Then listen and check.**

www.sydneyglobalhighschool.com

ABOUT
NEWS
STUDENTS
CONTACT
TEACHERS

Meet the New Students in Our School

Hi! I[1]'m .... Joana Silva. I[2] .... 12 years old and I[3] .... in Grade 7. I[4] .... from Australia. I'm from Brazil, but I[5] .... in Sydney with my family now. My parents [6] .... from Brazil, too. I have a sister and we do a lot of things together. Our favorite hobby [7] .... surfing. I love languages, and my favorite school subjects [8] .... English and Spanish.

3 **Put the words in the correct order to make questions.**

1 old / Are / 12 / you / years / ?
Are you 12 years old?

2 you / Russia / Are / from / ?
....

3 school / big / your / Is / ?
....

4 your / nice / Are / teachers / ?
....

LOOK!

I am Mexican. = I'm Mexican.

She is not Mexican. =
She's not Mexican. / She isn't Mexican.

You are not Mexican. =
You're not Mexican. / You aren't Mexican.

USE IT!

4 **Work in pairs. Ask and answer the questions in Exercise 3.**

CAN FOR ABILITY

1 0.04 **Complete the sentences. Use the correct form of *can* and the verbs. Then listen and check.**

1 Sarah ....can ice-skate.... (ice-skate) very well. (+)
2 My grandparents .... (play) video games. (–)
3 .... you .... (ski)? (?)
4 I .... (dance) the samba. (–)
5 .... your parents .... (run) 10 km? (?)
6 My friends and I .... (speak) English. (+)

IN, ON, AT

2 Complete the chart. Use *in*, *on*, and *at*.

We use ...	with ...
1	time (7 o'clock, 7 p.m.)
2	months (March), years (2030)
3	days of the week (Monday)

3 Complete the sentences with *in*, *on*, or *at*. Check (✓) the sentences that are true for you. Then tell a partner.

1 I go to the science lab ....on.... Wednesdays.
2 My birthday isn't .... May.
3 I go to bed .... 10:15 .... Saturdays.
4 I have dinner .... 7 o'clock every day.

SIMPLE PRESENT

4 Read Mia's plans for the week. Write *T* (true) or *F* (false). Then correct the false sentences.

Weekly Planner

Monday	Tuesday	Wednesday	Thursday	Friday
First day of school. Take Bus 22.	*Buy blue vase for Mom after school.*	*Mom's birthday. Party at 7 p.m.* 🙂❤❤❤	*Movies at Pat's house. My house next week!*	*Music practice 6 p.m. every week!*

1 Mia has a party on Thursday. ....F....
....She doesn't have a party on Thursday. She has a party on Wednesday....
2 She practices music on Fridays. ....
....
3 She watches movies on Thursdays. ....
....
4 Her mom hates blue. ....
....
5 She walks to school. ....
....

USE IT!

5 Work in pairs. Talk about what you do every week.

I play soccer on Saturdays.
That's nice!
I hang out with my friends on Sundays.
Me too.

1 **Complete the questions with *Do* or *Does*. Then ask and answer with a partner.**

1 ....Do.......... you have computer science classes?
2 .... your friend watch movies at your house?
3 .... you like cold pizza?
4 .... your cousins go to bed early on Saturdays?
5 .... you and your friends do your homework at school?
6 .... your English teacher wear glasses?

CLOTHES

2 0.05 **Complete the clothes words. Then listen, check, and repeat.**

1 
2 
3 
4 
5 
6 

s...weatshirt... j.................... d.................... s.................... s.................... s....................

PRESENT PROGRESSIVE

3 **Look at the image. Complete the sentences with the correct affirmative (+) or negative (–) form of the present progressive.**

Beatriz Leonardo Isaac Laura Theo

1 Beatriz ....is wearing......... a skirt.
2 Beatriz and Theo .... sneakers.
3 Laura .... glasses.
4 Leonardo .... shorts.
5 Isaac and Theo .... pants.
6 Isaac is saying: "I .... a blue T-shirt."

LOOK!

We add *–ing* to the verb in the present progressive:
***wear* → *wearing*; *take* → *taking*; *swim* → *swimming*.**

USE IT!

4 **Work in pairs. Take turns describing a classmate for your partner to guess.**

She's wearing blue jeans and a red T-shirt.

Is it Marina?

No, it's not!

PRESENT PROGRESSIVE

1 **Write questions about the teenagers in the image. Then ask and answer the questions with a partner.**

1 Sophia and Evelyn / talk / ?
Are Sophia and Evelyn talking?

2 Evelyn / wear / jeans / ?
....

3 Jessica / watch / TV / ?
....

4 Noah and Samuel / read / book / ?
....

5 Sophia and Evelyn / sit / on the sofa / ?
....

Are Sophia and Evelyn talking?

Yes, they are.

PRESENT PROGRESSIVE AND SIMPLE PRESENT

2 0.06 **Circle the correct options. Then listen and check.**

1 Sarah *wears* / *is wearing* red shoes today.
2 Mark *likes* / *is liking* sports.
3 My friends and I *are not sitting down* / *don't sit down* all day on the weekends.
4 *Do you go* / *Are you going* to restaurants on Saturdays?
5 My friend and I *talk* / *are talking* on the phone now.
6 *Is your teacher writing* / *Does your teacher write* on the board now?

3 **Complete the sentences so they are true for you.**

1 I ....like.... (like) pizza.
2 I .... (look) at my cell phone now.
3 I .... (have) a lot of cousins.
4 I .... (wear) jeans now.
5 I .... (do) my homework on Saturday evenings.

USE IT!

4 **Make questions from the sentences in Exercise 3. Ask and answer with a partner.**

Do you like pizza?

Yes, I do.

1 AROUND TOWN

UNIT GOALS

- Talk about places in town.
- Read about unusual towns.
- Listen to a dialogue.
- Learn about a festival.
- Speak about giving directions.

THINK!

1 Where are the teenagers in the photos?

2 Is it important to have places in town where teenagers can hang out? Why / Why not?

VIDEO

1.1

1 What things that change do you see?

2 Which four cities are in the video?

VOCABULARY IN CONTEXT

PLACES IN TOWN

1 1.01 **Complete the posts with the words below. Then listen and check.**

- bowling alley
- clothing store
- grocery store
- mall
- movie theater
- park
- ~~skatepark~~
- stadium

1

16:54

#I ❤ my neighborhood

Avava34

Western Park: the place to be with friends. There is a ....skatepark.......... in the ....!

2

17:14

My favorite places

SuperSonic

I love movies. The .... is my favorite place. It's in the .... ❤

3

13:32

My new neighborhood

Sooophil

I love my new neighborhood. There is a ....

We have a great sports ...., too!

4

9:26

My fave stores

Fun.Tastic

I go to the .... a lot with my dad to buy food. There is a lot of organic stuff there. And there's a nice .... next to it!

2 1.02 **Write the answers to the questions using words from Exercise 1. Then listen, check, and repeat.**

Where do you go to ...

1 buy jeans or a T-shirt? clothing store
2 buy stuff and have a snack with friends? ....
3 buy fruit, vegetables, and other kinds of food? ....
4 hang out with friends, run, or relax? ....
5 watch a soccer game? ....
6 see your favorite actor? ....
7 go bowling with friends or family? ....
8 hang out with friends and skate? ....

3 **Match the comments a–f with the posts 1–4 on page 10.**

a Where's that? Do they have organic yogurt there, too? 4
b 👍 That's my favorite place, too. Soccer is my life. ....
c Looks nice, but I don't have a skateboard 😔. ....
d I go there every weekend. I like the stores on the first floor. They're awesome! ....
e You're right. It's really cool. I love their jeans. ....
f I 💚 that place! My friends and I like to listen to music under the 🌲🌲🌲. ....

4 **Choose five words from Exercise 1 and write them in the chart. Then write three more places in town in the chart. You can use a dictionary.**

I go there with my family	I go there with my friends
....	....
....	....
....	....
....	....

USE IT!

5 **Look at your chart. Ask and answer questions in pairs. Circle the places in Exercise 4 where you and your partner both go.**

Do you go to the stadium with your family?

Yes, I do. Do you go to the park with your friends?

READING

www.unusualtowns.myblog

home | about me | **posts** | contact me

Whittier, Alaska, USA

Whittier is an unusual town because all its residents (around 200 people) live in the same building. There isn't a mall in Whittier, but there is a small grocery store there. In the building, you can also find a hotel, a restaurant, and a school. You get to the school through a tunnel under the ground. Why? Because it's very cold in Alaska! Read more

Thames Town, China

The River Thames is in England, so Thames Town is an English town, right? No, that's wrong. It is in China, near Shanghai, but the streets and stores look English. The street names are also in English: Oxford Street, Chelsea Street. There are red telephone boxes on the streets, and you can see a statue of Harry Potter there! Read more

1 **Look at the text, the title, and the images. Then complete the sentences with the phrases below.**

- about me
- blog posts
- unusual towns

The text shows two [1] .... about [2] .... To read about the author of the text, you have to click on [3] ....

2 1.03 **Read and listen to the text. Where can we find 1–5? Write *W* (Whittier) or *TT* (Thames Town).**

1 a statue ....
2 a grocery store ....
3 a tunnel to go to school ....
4 a street called Chelsea ....
5 a hotel ....

3 **Where is this image? Write *Whittier* or *Thames Town*.**

....

4 **Write *T* (true) or *F* (false).**

1 Whittier is an American town. ....
2 There are 200 buildings in Whittier. ....
3 The restaurant and the grocery store in Whittier are in the same building. ....
4 Thames Town is a Chinese neighborhood in England. ....
5 There are red streets in Thames Town. ....
6 The streets in Thames Town have English names. ....

THINK!

Imagine you live in Whittier. Then imagine you live in Thames Town. Which do you prefer? Why?

WORKBOOK p.115

LANGUAGE IN CONTEXT

1 **Look at the examples below. Complete the sentences from the blog post.**

There is/are				
Affirmative (+)	**Negative (–)**	***Yes/No* Questions (?)**	**Short Answers**	
There is a small grocery store in Whittier.	1 .... a mall in Whittier.	**Is there** a school in Whittier?	Yes, **there is**.	No, **there's not**. / No, **there isn't**.
2 .... red telephone boxes.	**There aren't** stadiums in Thames Town.	**Are there** stadiums in Whittier?	Yes, **there are**.	No, **there aren't**.

2 **Read the questions in the chart again. Write the correct short answers.**

1 Is there a school in Whittier? ....

2 Are there stadiums in Whittier? ....

3 **Complete the sentences. Use the correct form of *There is/are* affirmative (+) or negative (–).**

1 ....There is.... a bowling alley in my neighborhood. (+)

2 .... a movie theater in Whittier. (–)

3 .... many clothing stores in this mall. (+)

4 .... a nice library in my town. (+)

5 .... Japanese restaurants near my house. (–)

6 .... a cafeteria in my school. (–)

LOOK!

Remember: we don't use the verb *have*. We use *There is* or *There's* for singular nouns, and *There are* for plural nouns.

There **is a mall**. / There **are two malls** in my neighborhood.

4 **Write questions about your partner's town. Use the phrases.**

1 (a movie theater?) ....Is there a movie theater in your town?....

2 (nice gyms?) ....Are there nice gyms?....

3 (Mexican restaurants?) ....

4 (a skatepark?) ....

5 (a bowling alley?) ....

6 (clothing stores?) ....

USE IT!

5 **Work in pairs. Ask and answer the questions in Exercise 4.**

Is there a movie theater in your town?

Yes, there is.

WORKBOOK p.112 and 114

LISTENING AND VOCABULARY

1 1.04 **Label the diagrams with the words/phrases below. Then listen, check, and repeat.**

• behind • between • ~~in front of~~ • inside • left • next to • right

1 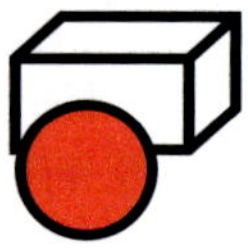
in front of

2 
....

3 
....

4 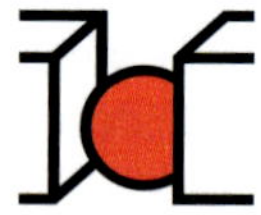
....

5 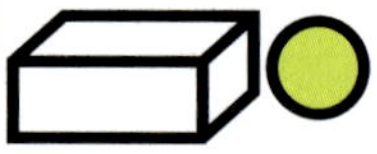
....

6 
....

7 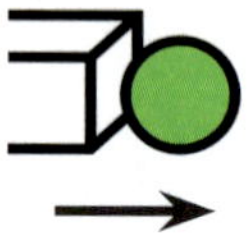
....

2 **Complete sentences 1–7 about the image. Use the correct words and phrases from Exercise 1.**

1 The bowling alley is on the ....left.... of the park.
2 The mall is on the .... of the park.
3 The grocery store is .... the mall.
4 The park is .... the bowling alley and the mall.
5 The restaurant is .... the mall.
6 There is a man .... the restaurant.
7 The restaurant is .... the man.

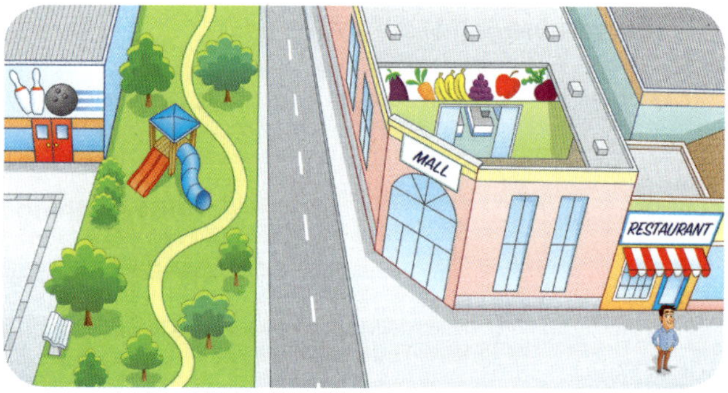

3 1.05 **Look at the images. Make predictions and answer the questions. Then listen and check.**

1 What are the girls talking about?
   a directions to a place ◯   b how to meet the boy ◯
2 Do the girls know the boy?
   a yes ◯   b no ◯

4 1.05 **Listen again. Complete sentences a–c. Then put them in the order you hear them (1–3).**

.... a We're here, ... Jefferson Street.
.... b Can you see that sign over .... ?
.... c I don't know where the movie theater ....

5 1.05 **Listen again and choose the correct route (A or B).**

A
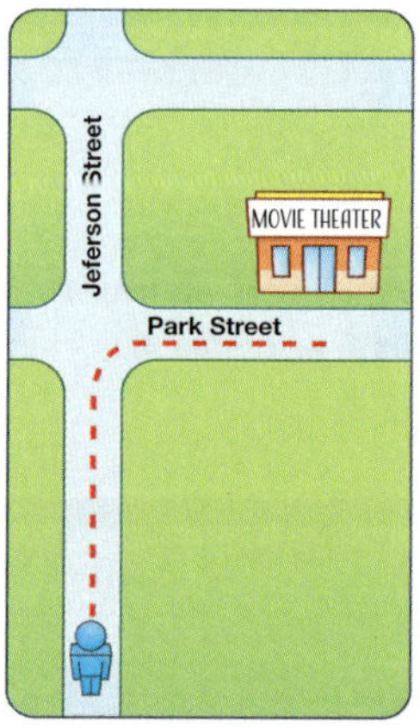

◯

B
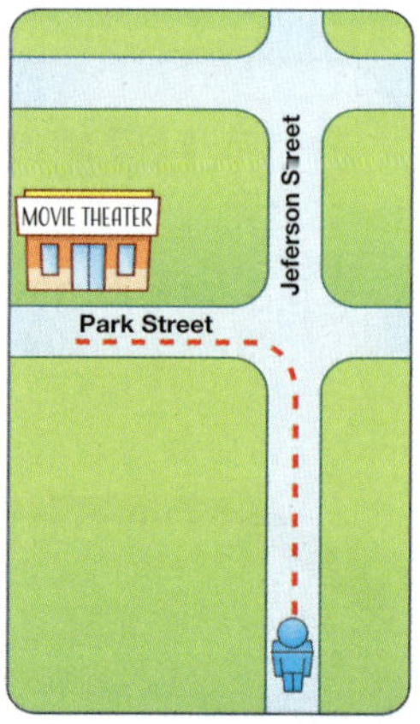

◯

LANGUAGE IN CONTEXT

1 **Complete the sentences from the dialogue in the chart. Use the phrases below.**

- always get
- never go

Adverbs of Frequency	
	How often do you go to the mall?
100% **Rosa** You [1]............................ lost.	I go to the mall **every day**.
Diego I **often** go to the movies.	I go to the mall **every weekend**.
Maria I **sometimes** go to the stadium.	I go to the mall **once/twice a month**.
0% **Maria** I [2]............................ to the movies.	I **never** go to the mall.

2 **Put the words in the correct order.**

1 friends / I / my / to / with / always / bowling / go / the / alley

I always go to the bowling alley with my friends.

2 with / sometimes / mall / out / her / at / Carolina / the / hangs / friends

....

3 often / TV / sister / evening / My / the / watches / in

....

4 to / My / never / Wednesdays / the / on / friends / go / skatepark

....

5 My / I / volleyball / school / brother / and / play / always / at

....

3 **Write questions with *How often* using the words/phrases.**

1 How often do you go to a restaurant? (go / restaurant)
2 ....? (hang out / skatepark)
3 ....? (watch / movies)
4 ....? (play / basketball)
5 ....? (drink / orange juice)
6 ....? (go / grocery store)

USE IT!

4 **Work in pairs. Ask and answer the questions from Exercise 3. Use adverbs of frequency in your answers.**

How often do you go to a restaurant?

I go to a restaurant once a month.

WORKBOOK p.112 and 113 PRACTICE EXTRA

AROUND THE WORLD

www.ateenwholovestowrite.blog.com

Home | Posts | About me

Beautiful Olinda

(in Portuguese, Olinda Linda)

I'm from Olinda, a town in Pernambuco State in Brazil. I love my town, and in this post I'm writing about Olinda again!

1 ________________

At this time of the year, it's Carnival time! There are street parties for 11 days and nights in Olinda. People listen to music and watch the parades. Frevo is a traditional dance in Pernambuco. I love it!

2 ________________

My mom is a cook. She sometimes works at Carnival. I always go to the Safe Zone for teens when she's working. I meet my friends and have snacks there. I often play video games there, too.

3 ________________

Do you like colors? Then Olinda is the place for you. There are great art museums, but you can see art in the streets, too. Olinda is fun!

4 ________________

Olinda is a UNESCO World Heritage Site. This means that the town is not only my Olinda: it's <u>your</u> Olinda, too!

REPLY

1 **Look at the text quickly. Then check (✓) the correct answers in the chart.**

What?	1 The text is:	◯ in an encyclopedia.	◯ a blog post.
	2 The topic of the text is:	◯ a town.	◯ Carnival.
Who?	3 The author of the text is:	◯ a teenager.	◯ an adult.
What for?	4 The objective of the text is to give:	◯ directions.	◯ information.

2 1.06 **Write the headings in the correct place in the text (1–4). Then read, listen, and check.**

A Place For Teens | Art Is Everywhere | It's Carnival Time | Our Olinda

3 **The text says: "I love my town, and in this post I'm writing about Olinda again!" What does this mean? Circle the correct options.**

1 The blog's author *lives* / *doesn't live* in Olinda.

2 This *is* / *isn't* the author's first blog about Olinda.

WORDS IN CONTEXT

4 **Look at the words in bold. Then match 1–4 with a–d.**

1 I love samba school **parades**. ....

2 My grandmother is a great **cook**. ....

3 Be **safe** during Carnival. ....

4 I don't have **snacks** at the stadium. ....

a Don't talk to people you don't know.

b There is a famous one in Rio.

c I prefer to go to a restaurant after the game.

d I love to have dinner at her house.

5 **Read the text again and complete the sentences.**

1 People celebrate Carnival in Olinda …
  a from Saturday to Wednesday. ◯
  b for more than a week. ✓

2 The author goes to the Safe Zone …
  a every day. ◯
  b during Carnival. ◯

3 In the Safe Zone, …
  a teenagers can hang out with their friends. ◯
  b teenagers can have science lessons. ◯

4 The author of the text thinks that the art museums in Olinda are …
  a nice. ◯
  b big. ◯

5 In "it's your Olinda, too!", *your* refers to …
  a the people from Olinda. ◯
  b the reader. ◯

THINK!

Do you feel safe during Carnival? Why / Why not? What do you think about the safe area for teens in Olinda?

WEBQUEST

Learn more! Check (✓) *True* or *False*.

Olinda is the only UNESCO World Heritage Site in Brazil.

◯ **True** ◯ **False**

VIDEO

1.2

1 Why do people celebrate Children's Day?

2 Which three countries are in the video?

SPEAKING

GIVING DIRECTIONS

1 1.07 **Read and listen to Olivia and Benjamin. What's the problem?**

Olivia Hey, **Benjamin**. Are you OK?
Benjamin Yeah ... But I can't find the **bowling alley**.
Olivia Where are you?
Benjamin Let me see. I'm on **Nevada Street, in front of the park**.
Olivia OK. Go straight, then turn **right on Main Street**.
Benjamin OK ...
Olivia The **bowling alley** is **next to the mall**.
Benjamin Oh, I see. Thanks! I'm on my way.

LIVING ENGLISH

2 Complete the mini dialogues with the expressions below.

• Are you OK? • I'm on my way. • Let me see.

1 A What time is it?
B .... It's 7:15.

2 A Are you coming?
B I'm in the car. ....

3 A I have a problem.
B What's your problem? ....

3 1.08 **Listen and repeat the expressions.**

PRONUNCIATION

4 1.09 **Listen and repeat the questions. Notice the intonation.**

Where are ↘ you?

Are you ↗ OK?

5 1.07 **Listen to the dialogue again. Then practice with a partner.**

6 Role play a new dialogue. Follow the steps.

1 Choose to start from A (you want to go to the movie theater) or B (you want to go to the grocery store).
2 Change the words in **blue** in Exercise 1 to write a new dialogue in your notebook asking directions to the movie theater or grocery store.
3 Practice your dialogue with a partner.
4 Present your dialogue to the class.

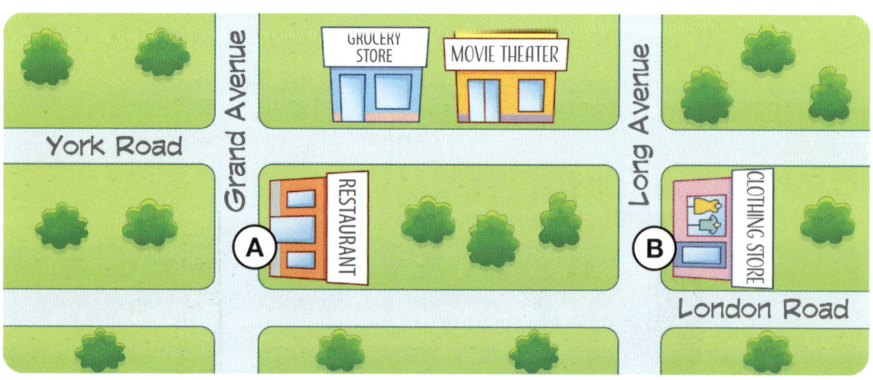

YOUR DIGITAL PORTFOLIO

Record your dialogue and upload it to your class digital portfolio.

PRACTICE EXTRA

2 DELICIOUS DIVERSITY

UNIT GOALS

- Talk about food.
- Read about students' lunchtimes in two countries.
- Listen to a TV cooking show.
- Learn about how to have a healthy diet.
- Write a recipe.

THINK!

1 Where do you normally eat?

2 Give three reasons why people eat together.

VIDEO

2.1

1 How many different types of bread are in the video?

2 Say two types of bread that you see.

VOCABULARY IN CONTEXT

FOOD

1 2.01 **Read the school lunch menu. Use the words in bold to label images 1–8. Then listen, check, and repeat.**

Varietas Middle School

Lunch Menu

Monday, September 7

Let's celebrate the independence of Brazil with a traditional lunch!

Brazilian Delight

- **Carrot** salad with **cheese**
- **Rice** and **beans** with **chicken** or **fish**
- **Pineapple**

Drink: **orange juice**

1 beans

2 ....

3 ....

4 ....

5 ....

6 ....

7 ....

8 ....

2 Write the correct food and drink under the headings on the tray.

• ~~beans~~ • carrot • cheese • chicken • fish • orange juice • pineapple • rice

3 2.02 Listen to the conversations and check (✓) the correct image.

1 A  B 

2 A  B 

3 A  B 

4 A  B 

USE IT!

4 Work in pairs. Ask and answer the question: What do you like to eat and drink? Complete the diagram.

I like ...	We both like ...	My classmate likes ...

READING

www.teeninfomag.net

SCHOOL LIFE

What's for lunch today?

by Taylor Ramirez, Monday, March 4

Students have lunch at school every day. Read and find out what they eat in two countries!

"*Hei* from Finland! School lunches are free, but delicious! Today I'm having fish, potatoes, and carrot salad. I love lunchtime because I can hang out with my friends!"
Olavi, 12

WOW! facts:

- Students can't take food to school.
- Students can have a free lunch in the park during vacation.

"Hi there! Here in South Korea we have lunch with our teachers! Today I'm having fish soup, rice, and *kimchi*, a traditional dish with vegetables. I love it!"
Seo-Yoon, 13

WOW! facts:

- Students clean the tables after lunch.
- In many schools, there aren't drinks during lunch.

Do you have lunch at school? What is it like? Tell us at tramirez@teeninfomag.net.

1 Look at the article. What is it about?

○ Life in Finland and South Korea. ○ School food in Finland and South Korea.

2 Check (✓) all the elements that you see in the article.

- ✓ a title
- ○ the journalist's name
- ○ the date
- ○ a graph
- ○ images
- ○ comments from readers

3 2.03 Read and listen to the article. Then read the sentences and write *F* (Finland), *SK* (South Korea), or *B* (both).

1 Students don't pay for school lunches. F
2 Students and teachers eat together. ______
3 Students eat vegetables at school. ______
4 There is free lunch for students at parks. ______
5 Students can't take lunch to school. ______
6 Students clean tables after lunch. ______

4 Read the article again. What do Olavi and Seo-Yoon love?

Olavi ______________________________

Seo-Yoon ______________________________

THINK!

In South Korea, students clean the tables after lunch. Think about your school. Who cleans it? How do you help to keep it clean?

WORKBOOK p.119

LANGUAGE IN CONTEXT

1 **Look at the examples below. Complete the sentences from the online article.**

***Can* for Permission (I, You, He/She/It, We, They)**		
Affirmative (+)	**Negative (–)**	***Yes/No* Questions (?) and Short Answers**
I **can hang out** with my friends.	Students [1]............................ take food to school.	**Can** I **drink** juice at lunch time? Yes, I **can**. / No, I **can't**. [2]............................ you **take** food to school? Yes, you **can**. / No, you **can't**.

2 **Complete the sentences. Use the correct form of *can* and the verbs.**

1 At Julia's school, students ....can't listen........ (listen) to music in class. (–)
2 After school, I .... (play) video games before I do my homework. (+)
3 Melissa .... (eat) in the classroom at her school. (–)
4 My classmates and I .... (have) breakfast at school. (+)
5 Students .... (have) dinner at school in South Korea. (+)
6 Mateus .... (eat) fish. He is allergic to it. (–)

3 **Write questions about what you can do at home. Use *can* and the phrases.**

1 (go to bed after 10 p.m. on weekdays?)
........Can you go to bed after 10 p.m. on weekdays?........
2 (eat chocolate every day?)
....
3 (have dinner in your bedroom?)
....
4 (play video games in the evenings?)
....
5 (use your cell phone during meals?)
....
6 (do homework on your bed?)
....

USE IT!

4 **Work in pairs. Ask and answer the questions in Exercise 3.**

Can you go to bed after 10 p.m. on weekdays?

Yes, I can.

LISTENING AND VOCABULARY

1 2.04 **Put the letters in the correct order and write the words about cooking. Then listen, check, and repeat.**

COOKING			
Food		**Utensils**	
 1 salt (tlas)	 2 .... (nooin)	 3 .... (frko)	 4 .... (enifk)
Actions			
 5 .... salt. (dad)	 6 .... the fish. (utc)	 7 .... the fish. (yrf)	 8 .... the eggs. (ixm)

2 2.05 **Listen to the first part of a TV show. Check (✓) the best title.**

○ 

○ 

○ 

3 2.05 **Listen again and circle the correct options.**

1 The participants have *carrots and fish* / *rice and beans* / *fish and rice* to make a dish.
2 They decide to make a *Brazilian* / *Korean* / *Mexican* dish.

4 2.06 **Listen to the second part of the TV show. Number the sentences in the order you hear them.**

a A Korean dish! Nice! And how do you make it? ....
b Chef Jessica is coming ... don't look at her! 1
c Don't forget to add salt to the eggs. ....
d First we cut the fish with this special knife. ....
e It sounds delicious! Good luck! ....
f Then we mix the eggs. ....

WORKBOOK p.116 and 117

LANGUAGE IN CONTEXT

1 Complete the sentences from the TV show in the chart. Use the words/phrases below.

• Why don't I • Let's • How about

Making Suggestions and Responding

A [1] .... making a Korean dish?
B **Great idea**! / **Well**, I prefer Mexican food.
A [2] .... make saeng sun jun!
B **Good idea**!
A [3] .... cut the fish?
B **Sure**! / **Don't worry**, I can do that.

LOOK!

Remember to use the *-ing* form of the verb after *How about / What about*.

2 Write suggestions. Use the words/phrases.

1 have lunch together (let's)
Let's have lunch together!
2 have pizza for dinner (how about)
....
3 cut some carrots for a salad (why don't I)
....
4 make eggs for breakfast (let's)
....
5 do homework together (how about)
....
6 play volleyball after class (let's)
....

3 Look at the words in bold in the sentences from the TV show. Then complete the chart with the correct object pronouns.

Subject and Object Pronouns

a **Olivia** Why don't **I** cut the fish?
James Please pass **me** the eggs.
b **Olivia** Chef Jessica is coming ... don't look at **her**!
c **Olivia** Let's make saeng sun jun! **It**'s fried fish – **it** is simple and delicious!
James We can serve **it** with rice!
d **Olivia** Then we mix the eggs.
Chef Jessica Use a fork to mix **them**, OK?

Subject pronouns	Object pronouns
I	[1] me
you	you
he	him
she	[2] ....
it	[3] ....
we	us
they	[4] ....

LOOK!

Never omit object pronouns.
Cut the fish and then fry **it**.

4 Replace the words in bold with an object pronoun.

1 I don't watch ~~**MasterCook**~~. it
2 Can you cut **the carrots**? ....
3 Sofia likes **James**. ....
4 Chef Jessica talks with **Sofia and James**. ....
5 Miguel goes to school with **you and Bruno**. ....
6 Please pass the eggs to **Amelia**. ....

USE IT!

Let's have lunch together!

Great idea!

5 Work in pairs. Take turns making the suggestions in Exercise 2 and responding to them.

WORKBOOK p.116 and 118 PRACTICE EXTRA

ACROSS THE CURRICULUM

SCIENCE

Tips for a Healthy Diet

1

Eat natural food

Natural food is all around us: fruit, vegetables, eggs … they have a lot of nutrients and keep us healthy.

2

Be careful with oil, salt, and sugar

They help make food delicious, but remember to use them in small amounts.

3

Be careful with processed food, and avoid ultra-processed food

Processed food has ingredients that are not good for us. Look at some examples.

Natural food	Processed food	Ultra-processed food
 fresh orange juice	 orange juice in a carton	 soft drink with orange flavor
 chicken	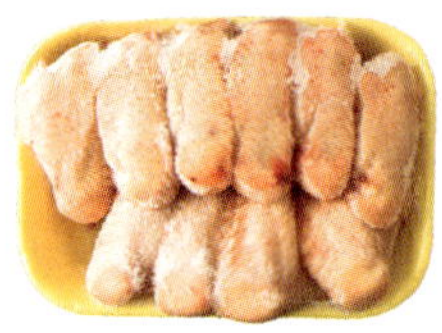 frozen chicken	 chicken nuggets

4

Eat at regular times with company

It is important to eat slowly in a quiet place – and don't check your cell phone! Also, it is always more fun to have meals with family, friends, or classmates.

5

Eat a variety of food

Add color to your plate. Check that you always eat some carbohydrates, protein, fruit, and vegetables every day. Variety is good for you.

6

Have a meat-free day

How often do you eat meat? It's not healthy or necessary to eat meat for every meal. How about being vegetarian for one day a week?

1 **Look at the infographic and check (✓) the correct option.**

◯ It's short and informative. ◯ It's long and it tells a story.

2 2.07 **Read and listen to the text. Write *T* (true) or *F* (false).**

1 Fruit and vegetables are healthy. T
2 It's positive to eat lots of oil, salt, and sugar. ....
3 Chicken nuggets are an example of ultra-processed food. ....
4 Eating with a friend is good for you. ....
5 Eating different types of food isn't good for you. ....
6 On a meat-free day, you can eat chicken. ....

3 **Read about the eating habits of six different people. Match them with tips 1–6 in the infographic.**

a "I usually have salad, rice, beans, and chicken for lunch." 5
b "I never drink soda or eat chicken nuggets." ....
c "I never use my cell phone during dinner time." ....
d "I don't add salt to my food or sugar to my coffee." ....
e "I don't eat meat on Mondays." ....
f "I always include fruit and vegetables in my meals." ....

WORDS IN CONTEXT

4 **Look at the words in bold. Then match 1–4 with a–d.**

1 Vegetables are **healthy**. ....
2 Mike and Lucas **avoid** ultra-processed food. ....
3 Anna and Luisa eat **slowly**. ....
4 The Taylors don't eat **meat** on Thursdays. ....

a They try not to eat chicken nuggets.
b They take 45 minutes to eat a salad!
c They don't eat chicken or fish on this day.
d They are good for your body.

THINK!

Do you think that it is a good idea to have a meat-free day every week? Why / Why not?

WEBQUEST

Learn more! Check (✓) *True* or *False*.

White chocolate is not chocolate.

◯ **True** ◯ **False**

VIDEO

2.2

1 **What Mediterranean countries are in the video?**
2 **Say two foods that you see.**

WRITING

1 **Look at the recipe. What is it for? Complete the title with *a* or *b*.**

a Chicken and Rice Special
b Fish and Rice Special

One-pot ....

◆ **Preparation time: 30 minutes**

◆ 1 Ingredients

2 carrots
2 tbsp. of oil
salt
2 cups of rice
½ onion
8 cups of water
chicken

◆ 2 ....

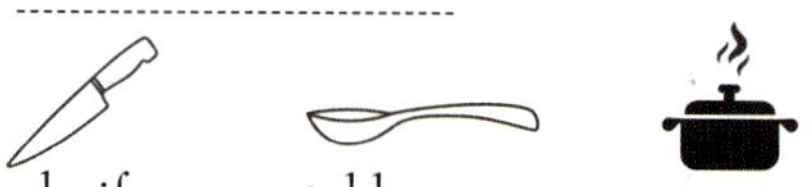

knife tablespoon pot

◆ 3 ....

1. 4 .... the carrots, onion, and chicken. Add salt to the chicken.
2. Put the oil in a pot and 5 .... the carrots for 5–6 minutes.
3. Then 6 .... the rice and onion. Fry them for one minute.
4. Next, add the chicken and the water. 7 .... for 10–15 minutes.

Enjoy your meal!

2 **Complete the recipe with the headings and the instruction words below.**

Headings	Instruction words
• ~~Ingredients~~ • Instructions • Utensils	• add • cook • cut • fry

3 2.08 **Read and listen to the recipe. Check your answers to Exercises 1 and 2.**

4 **Write a recipe.**

1 Choose a dish you like.
2 Collect information about the ingredients, utensils, and instructions.
3 Find or draw an image to illustrate the recipe.
4 Write the first version of your recipe. Use vocabulary from the unit.

LOOK!

Use the imperative to give instructions in recipes.

Cut the onion.

Fry the chicken.

5 **Switch your recipe with a partner, and check his/her work. Use the checklist below.**

○ title
○ clear sections: ingredients, utensils, and instructions
○ clear instructions in the imperative

YOUR DIGITAL PORTFOLIO

Edit your recipe, then publish it. Upload it to the class portfolio for everyone to see!

REVIEW
UNITS 1 AND 2

VOCABULARY

1 Put the letters in the correct order and write the words/phrases. Then match sentences 1–4 with images A–D.

1 I have an idea. Let's go to the .... (eomiv tarhtee)!
2 My parents buy vegetables and fruit at this .... (rgoeycr tesro).
3 Do you have a skateboard? There's a nice .... (ksarekpta) near here.
4 I often go to the .... (utsmida) with my parents on Sundays. I love sports.

A 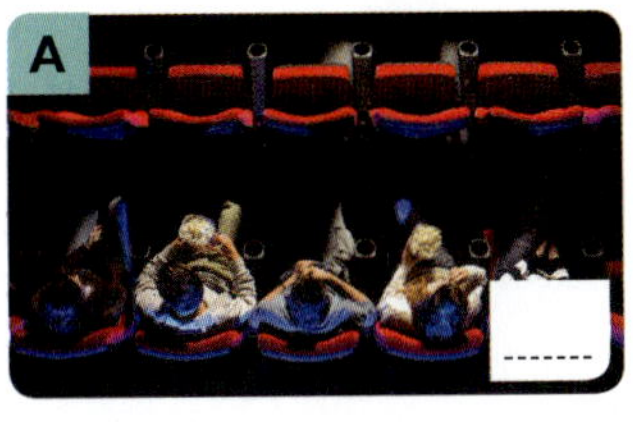 ....

B  ....

C  ....

D  ....

2 Label the images with the ingredients. Use the words below. Then check (✓) your favorite dish.

• beans • carrots • cheese • ~~chicken~~ • fish • pineapple • rice

1 

chicken
....
....

2 

....
....

3 

....
....

3 Circle the one that doesn't belong. Then complete sentences a–d with the correct circled words (1–4).

1 onion / salt / fork
2 fry / chicken / cheese
3 rice / knife / beans
4 add / mix / carrots

a Do you use your hands or a ....fork.... to eat pizza?
b I need a .... to cut this chicken.
c Why don't I .... the fish?
d I love .... in salad, don't you?

4 Look at the image and complete the sentences. Use the words/phrases below.

• ~~behind~~ • between • in front of
• inside • next to

1 The carrots are ....behind.... the onions.
2 The orange juice is .... the water.
3 The onions are .... the carrots.
4 The rice is .... the beans and the salt.
5 The carrots and onions are .... a box.

LANGUAGE IN CONTEXT

5 **Complete the sentences with *There is/are* in the correct affirmative (+), negative (–), or question (?) forms.**

1 .... clothing stores in this neighborhood? (?)
2 .... nice parks near my house. (–)
3 .... chicken for lunch today. (+)
4 .... a movie theater in this town? (?)

6 **Look at some of Liz's eating habits. Then complete the sentences with the words below.**

• always • often • sometimes • never

	Mon	Tue	Wed	Thu	Fri	Sat	Sun
Have beans for lunch	✓	✓	✓	✓	✓	✓	✓
Have rice with eggs	✓	✓	✓	✓	✓		
Eat fish with carrots		✓		✓			
Add salt to food							

1 Liz .... eats fish with carrots.
2 She .... adds salt to her food.
3 She .... has beans for lunch.
4 She .... has rice with eggs.

7 **Match the questions 1–4 with the answers a–d.**

1 Can I open the window? ....
2 Can I have lunch at school? ....
3 Can I have a soda? ....
4 Can I go to the park with my friends? ....

a No, stay home and do your homework.
b No, it's cold in here!
c Yes, but don't eat junk food.
d Yes, they're in the fridge. But just one!

8 **Circle the correct options.**

Alicia Is there a restaurant near here?
Jorge I don't know. There's a woman over there. I can ask [1]*she* / *her*. Excuse me. Can you help [2]*us* / *we*? Is there a restaurant near here?
Ana Mmm … Yes! Can you see the mall over there?
Jorge Yes, I can see [3]*it* / *him*.
Ana There are two restaurants in the mall: a Japanese one and an Italian one. [4]*They* / *Them* are very good.
Alicia That's great! [5]*We* / *Us* love Japanese food. Thanks!

CHECK YOUR PROGRESS

I CAN ...

- talk about places in town
- use *there is/are* and adverbs of frequency
- talk about food
- use *can* for permission, make and respond to suggestions, and use subject and object pronouns.

LEARN TO LEARN

Finding the right meaning in a dictionary

Some words have more than one meaning. You can look at the grammar function in the dictionary to find the correct meaning.

James and Sofia <u>cook</u> a Korean dish.

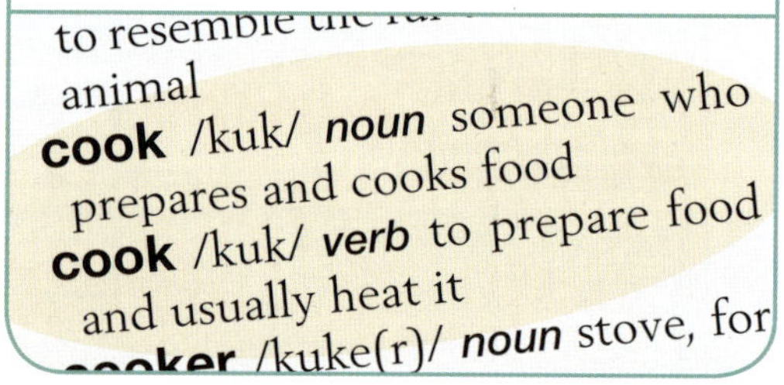

3 **Write the correct words/phrases for the icons on the map.**

- amusement park
- beach
- camping
- country
- historic center
- ~~museum~~
- sightseeing
- street market

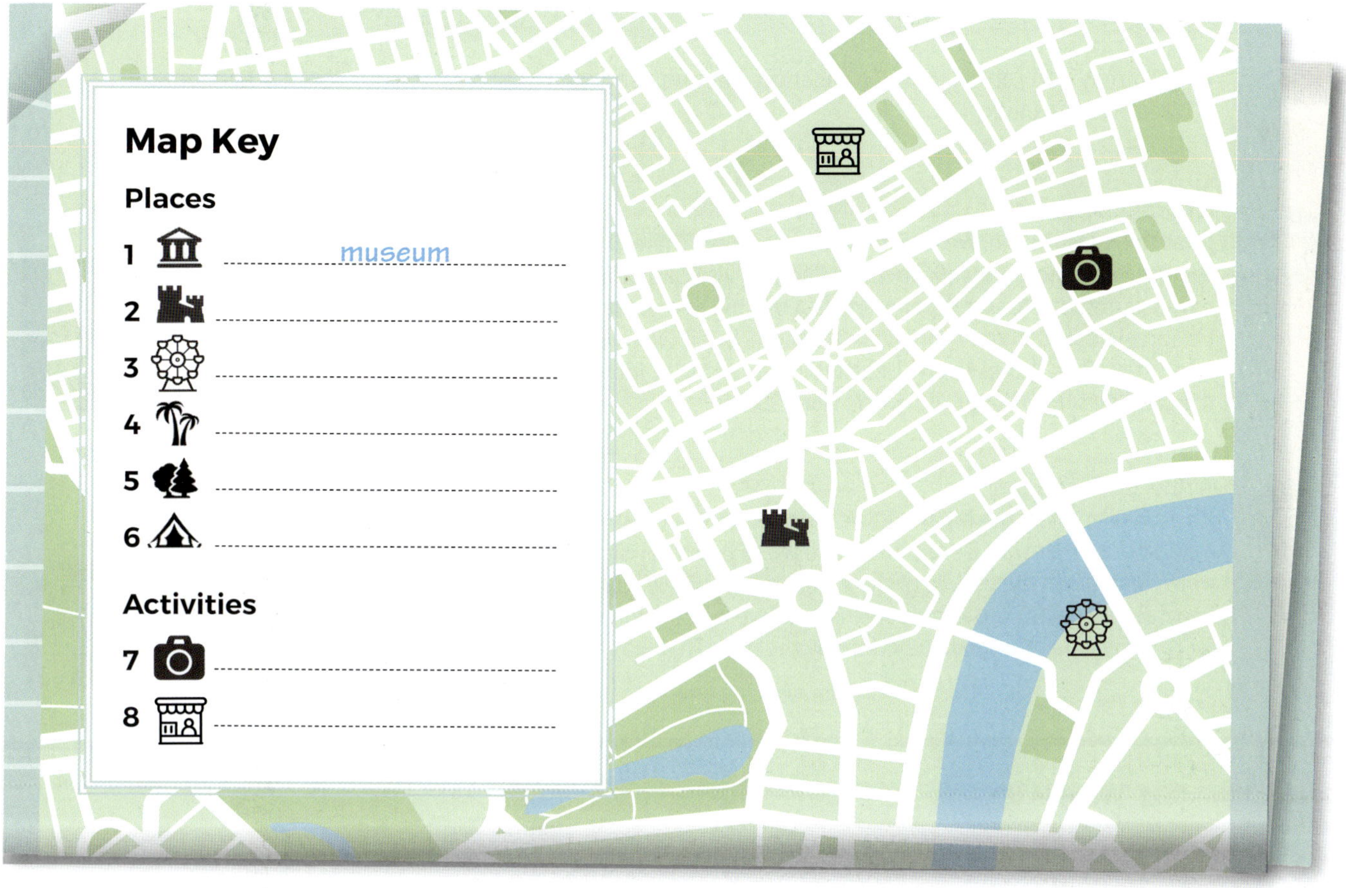

4 **Look at vacation activities 1–4 in the chart and complete activities 5 and 6 with your own ideas. Then check (✓) the columns with your opinions.**

Vacation Activities	I love ... ❤❤❤	I like ... ❤	I don't like ... 💔
1 visiting museums			
2 swimming			
3 playing video games			
4 going to the beach			
5 going to			
6 hanging out at			

USE IT!

I love visiting museums!

Me too!

5 **Work in pairs. Share your opinions from the chart in Exercise 4.**

READING

Teen Travel | Interest Forums | **Favorite Vacations**

Angelita

Q My family and I are planning a vacation, and we need ideas. Can you tell me about your favorite vacation destination?

Travelbug

A Barcelona, Spain
I was there last spring. We weren't at the beaches. There were so many things to see and do – walk down La Rambla, visit Sagrada Familia, go to museums, parks, and street markets. I'm a big soccer fan, so I was at FC Barcelona's stadium. There wasn't a game, but it was awesome! An interesting fact: there weren't beaches in Barcelona before 1992, and the sand was from Egypt – it wasn't from Spain!

45 minutes ago | REPLY |

Julia2010

A Alter do Chão, Brazil
It's a small town by the Tapajos River, in the Amazon forest – I was at my aunt's house there last December. There was a beautiful island across from the town in the middle of the Amazon – wow! We were at the beach every day! One day my cousins and I were in the forest, and there were some cute monkeys. They were by the river. That was really fun!

59 minutes ago | REPLY |

1 Look at the text. What is it?

○ an online forum ○ a magazine article

2 Write the names of the people from the text.

1 Who asks a question? ....

2 Who answers the question? ....

3 3.02 **Read and listen to the text. Write *T* (true) or *F* (false).**

1 The online forum is about favorite vacations. ....
2 Angelita is planning a vacation with friends. ....
3 TravelBug doesn't like soccer. ....
4 There were beaches in Barcelona in 1986. ....
5 Some of Julia2010's family live in Alter do Chão. ....
6 There were monkeys in the town. ....

4 Read the text again. Complete the diagram with the attractions below. Which attraction do Barcelona and Alter do Chão both have?

- beach
- forest
- island
- monkeys
- ~~museums~~
- parks
- river
- stadium
- street markets

Barcelona | Alter do Chão

museums ....
....
....
....

THINK!

Imagine you are Angelita. Which place do you want to visit – Barcelona or Alter do Chão? Why?

WORKBOOK p.123

LANGUAGE IN CONTEXT

1 **Look at the examples below. Complete the sentences from the online forum.**

Simple Past of *to be* (Affirmative and Negative)	
Affirmative (+)	**Negative (–)**
I [1] ....was.... at my aunt's house.	I **wasn't** in Barcelona in the summer.
You **were** in Alter do Chão with your family.	You **weren't** in Alter do Chão with your friends.
She **was** at the beach every day.	It [4] .... from Spain.
We [2] .... at the beach every day.	We [5] .... at the beaches.
They [3] .... by the river.	They **weren't** in the houses.

2 **Complete the sentences. Use the correct simple past form of *to be*.**

1 I wasn't at home last weekend. I ....was.... at my uncle's house.
2 Ren was sick last Monday. He .... at school.
3 The students weren't in the classroom for the art class. They .... at lunch.
4 We were in Barcelona last spring. We .... in Madrid.
5 Julia2010 wasn't in Belém in December. She .... in Alter do Chão.
6 The weather was warm in Barcelona last spring. It .... cold.

3 **Look at the examples below. Complete the sentences from the online forum.**

There was/were	
Affirmative (+)	**There** [1] .... a beautiful island across from the town. **There** [2] .... so many things to see and do.
Negative (–)	**There** [3] .... a game. **There** [4] .... beaches in Barcelona before 1992.

4 **Look at the information about Cedar Town. Write sentences about the town in the 1980s.**

	In the 1980s	**Now**
1 bowling alley	×	✓
2 historic center	✓	✓
3 beaches	✓	✓
4 amusement park	×	✓

1 ....
2 ....
3 ....
4 ....

USE IT!

5 **Where were you last weekend? Write three places in your notebook.**

6 **Work in pairs. Can you guess where your classmate was last weekend?**

You were at the beach last Saturday.

No, I wasn't. I was at the beach last Sunday.

WORKBOOK p.120 and 122 PRACTICE EXTRA

LISTENING AND VOCABULARY

1 3.03 **Label the images with the words/phrases below. Then listen, check, and repeat.**

- fishing
- horseback riding
- ~~hotel room~~
- kayaking
- receptionist
- safari
- swimming pool
- tour guide

1 hotel room

2 ....

3 ....

4 ....

5 ....

6 ....

7 ....

8 ....

2 3.04 **Complete the pamphlet with words/phrases from Exercise 1. Listen and check your answers.**

Come and stay at the Amazing Safari Hotel!

We offer adventure, comfort, and fun all in one place!

Stay in a big and comfortable [1] hotel room in the heart of a nature reserve! Relax by the [2] ....!

Our experienced [3] .... takes guests to see elephants, lions, and other animals on [4] ....

But that's not all! At the Amazing Safari Hotel, you can also go [5] .... and go [6] .... at the river!

Just talk to a [7] .... to make a reservation!

3 3.05 **Listen to a conversation. Check (✓) the word/phrase that completes each sentence.**

1 The conversation is part of a …
a TV show. ◯ b podcast. ◯

2 Lucas Montes is the …
a presenter. ◯ b guest. ◯

3 Camila Sanchez is the …
a presenter. ◯ b guest. ◯

4 The conversation is about a …
a camping vacation. ◯ b hotel vacation. ◯

4 3.05 **Listen again and complete the notes.**

Podcast title: [1] Teens on the Go

- Camila was in a safari [2] .... in Kenya last July.
- The [3] .... was her favorite activity – James, the [4] ...., was very good.
- There were lots of wild [5] .... on the reserve – giraffes, hippos, elephants, and lions.
- She wasn't afraid of the lions. In fact, the lions were her [6] .... animals.

WORKBOOK p.120 and 121

LANGUAGE IN CONTEXT

1 **Complete the questions from the conversation in the chart. Use *was* or *were*.**

Simple Past of *to be*: *Yes/No* Questions and Short Answers		
Was I afraid of the lions?	Yes, I **was**.	No, I **wasn't**.
1........................ you afraid of the lions?	Yes, you **were**.	No, you **weren't**.
2........................ the tour guide good?	Yes, he/she **was**.	No, he/she **wasn't**.
Were we afraid of the lions?	Yes, we **were**.	No, we **weren't**.
3........................ the other animals afraid of the lions?	Yes, they **were**.	No, they **weren't**.

2 **Look at the activities for the day at the Amazing Safari Hotel last July. Write questions and answers.**

Amazing Safari Hotel

Activities

7:30 a.m. – breakfast at the Masai Restaurant
8:15 a.m. – daytime safari with tour guide (James)
2 p.m. – kayaking at Amazing River
5 p.m. – fishing at Amazing River
6 p.m. to 7 p.m. – dinner by the fire
7:15 p.m. – night safari with tour guide (Makena)

1 breakfast / at the Masai Restaurant / was / ?
....
....
2 the guests / at Amazing River / were / at 2:30 p.m. / ?
....
....
3 were / in their hotel rooms / at 5:15 p.m. / the guests / ?
....
....
4 James / the tour guide / was / on the night safari / ?
....
....

3 **Complete the questions from the conversation in the chart. Use *was* or *were*.**

There was/were: *Yes/No* Questions and Short Answers	
A 1........................ **there** a tour guide on the safari? B Yes, **there was**. / No, **there wasn't**.	A 2........................ **there** wild animals on the reserve? B Yes, **there were**. / No, **there weren't**.

4 **Write questions about the facilities and the people at the Amazing Safari Hotel.**

1 two restaurants? (× one restaurant)
Were there two restaurants?
2 swimming pool? (✓)
....
3 two tour guides? (✓)
....
4 four receptionists? (× three receptionists)
....

USE IT!

5 **Write the answers to the questions in Exercise 4 in your notebook. Then ask and answer with a partner.**

Were there two restaurants?

No, there weren't. There was one.

WORKBOOK p.120 and 122 PRACTICE EXTRA

AROUND THE WORLD

A FAMILY ROAD TRIP THROUGH FRANCE IN OUR OLD CAMPER!

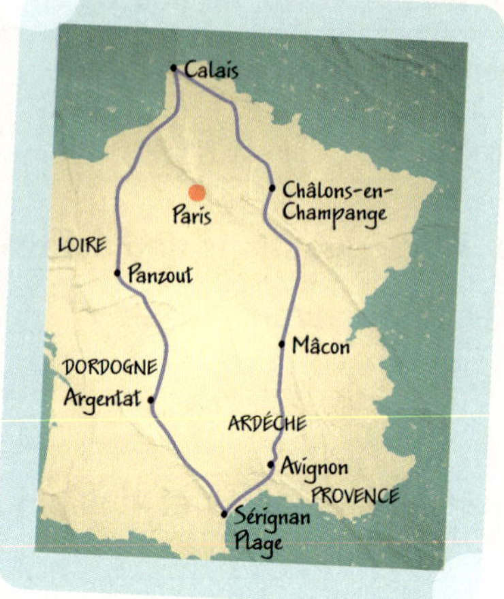

Mom, Dad, Elise, and I are traveling around France.

Day 7

This is our last day at the campground near Avignon, in Provence. We were in the city this morning – Dad was on Saint Benezet bridge – can you see him?

Dad

Day 8

The road trip through Provence was spectacular! The lavender is beautiful – look at all the colors! Even old Melinda was beautiful in the country.

Melinda

Day 10

Bonjour! Here we are at a campground at Sérignan beach. My sister Elise and I were at the beach all morning, sunbathing and swimming. There is a great bakery at the campground. Every morning we buy pastries for breakfast, and today we have baguettes for a picnic lunch!

Day 12

Say hello to the Loire Valley! There are bike paths everywhere – you can rent electric bikes and ride all day!

This is my mom by the Loire River after our bike ride. The Loire Valley was my favorite place this vacation.

1 **Look at Sophie's travel journal. Circle the correct options.**

1 It is about Sophie's trip *to Paris / around France.*
2 She was with her *friends / family.*
3 They travel by *bike / camper*.

2 3.06 **Read and listen to Sophie's travel journal. Check your ideas in Exercise 1.**

3 **Read the travel journal again. Check (✓) the sentence that is not correct.**

1 It is about a vacation around a country. ◯
2 It is organized into days. ◯
3 It combines text and images. ◯
4 It doesn't present Sophie's opinions about the places. ◯

4 **Number the events in Sophie's trip in order 1–6.**

.... a Bike ride around the Loire Valley
.... b Go swimming at the beach
.... c Picnic lunch
...1... d One week stay at a campground near Avignon
.... e Road trip through Provence
.... f Visit to the bridge in Avignon

WORDS IN CONTEXT

5 **Match the words 1–4 with their definitions a–d.**

1 bike path ....
2 campground ....
3 road trip ....
4 sunbathing ....

a long journey or vacation in a vehicle
b place where you can go camping on vacation
c special route for people to ride their bikes
d sitting or lying in the sun

THINK!

Imagine you are on a road trip in a camper with your family. What do you like? What don't you like?

WEBQUEST

Learn more! Check (✓) *True* or *False*.
Saint Benezet bridge doesn't get to the other side of the river.

◯ **True** ◯ **False**

VIDEO

3.2

1 Say two things you can do in Costa Rica.
2 What different animals do you see in the video?

SPEAKING

TALKING ABOUT YOUR VACATION

1 3.07 **Read and listen to Pedro and Mike. Where were they on vacation?**

Pedro Hey, **Mike**, how was your vacation?

Mike It was **great**! I was at a **campground at the beach**. You can **go swimming there**. What about you?

Pedro I was at my **grandparents' house in the country**.

Mike And how was it?

Pedro It was **cool**! There was **a big party in the town**.

Mike Awesome! That sounds fun!

LIVING ENGLISH

2 **Complete the mini dialogues with the expressions below.**

• Cool! • Hey, • What about you?

1 A My vacation was really nice!

B ....

2 A I was at home the whole summer.

....

B I was at my aunt's house in the country.

3 A .... Marina! Where were you?

B I was at the swimming pool.

3 3.08 **Listen and repeat the expressions.**

PRONUNCIATION

4 3.09 **Listen and repeat the compound nouns. Underline the stressed word or part of the word.**

1 <u>bike</u> path
2 campground
3 road trip
4 skatepark
5 street market
6 swimming pool

5 3.07 **Listen to the dialogue again. Then practice with a partner.**

6 **Role play a new dialogue. Follow the steps.**

1 Change the words in **blue** in Exercise 1 to write a new dialogue in your notebook.
2 Practice your dialogue with a partner.
3 Present your dialogue to the class.

YOUR DIGITAL PORTFOLIO

Record your dialogue and upload it to your class digital portfolio.

PRACTICE EXTRA

4 WE ALL HAVE A STORY

UNIT GOALS

- Talk about stories and storytelling.
- Read a story with a moral.
- Listen to a radio interview.
- Learn about storytelling.
- Write a story summary.

THINK!

1. Where is the teenager in the photo? What is he doing?
2. Why do you think people read stories?

VIDEO 4.1

1. What fun activity is the video about?
2. Which two countries are in the video?

VOCABULARY IN CONTEXT

STORY VERBS

1 **Read the first social media story post (1). Then read posts 2–6 and match them with the images (A–E).**

1

My day doesn't start very well. I look at my phone and **shout**, "I'm very late!" I **rush** out of my bedroom.

16: 54

2 ---------

I **arrive** at school and go to my classroom. There's nobody there.

16: 55

3 ---------

But I'm hungry and I **want** some food. I **walk** to the cafeteria.

16: 56

4 ---------

Then I **remember**! Today is our annual Science Fair. This year's topic is "Creativity".

16: 57

5 ---------

I use my cell all the time, so I **decide** to make a video about my day.

16: 58

6 ---------

I show my video at the fair. My teachers **tell** me, "That's very creative!" I **laugh**.

16: 59

A

B

C

D

E

2 4.01 **Put the letters in the correct order to make verbs. Complete the sentences. Then listen, check, and repeat.**

1 I never remember (mrermebe) the dates of school events, do you?
2 My parents always .... (letl) me, "It's important to read many books."
3 Do you .... (akwl) to school or do you take the bus?
4 Do you .... (ulhga) when you watch comedy movies? I do.
5 What's the first thing you do when you .... (rairev) at school?
6 Don't .... (htsuo) at your sister. That's not nice.
7 I often get up late on Monday mornings and then I .... (hrus) to school.
8 I can't .... (eddice) what book to read next.
9 What do you .... (atwn) to watch, a drama or an adventure movie?

3 **Complete the chart with the verbs below. Then add other verbs you know to the chart.**

- decide • laugh • remember • ~~rush~~ • shout • tell • walk • want

Things you do with your ...		
legs	**mouth**	**brain**
		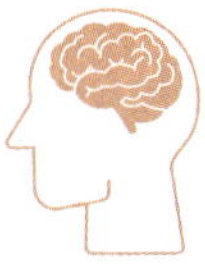
rush		

USE IT!

4 **Complete the chart for you. Write *Yes, I do*. or *No, I don't*. Then ask and answer in pairs. Write your partner's answers in the chart.**

	You	Your Partner
1 Do you walk to school?		
2 Do you remember to bring your gym clothes for PE class?		
3 Do you laugh when you play video games?		
4 Do you often arrive late at school?		
5 Do you want to go on a safari?		
6 Do you write stories on social media?		

5 **Write an affirmative (+) and a negative (–) sentence about your classmate. Then tell the class your sentences.**

Daniela walks to school.
She doesn't want to go on a safari. I do.

1 (+) ....
2 (–) ....

READING

Peter and the Wolf

1 A long time ago a man, a woman, and their son, Peter, lived on a farm near a village. Peter was 13 years old, and he often helped his father on the farm.

2 One day, Peter decided to have some fun. He shouted, "Wolf, wolf! Help!" The villagers rushed to help. When they arrived, they asked, "Peter, are you OK? Are the sheep OK? Where is the wolf?" Peter laughed and laughed. He answered, "There is no wolf. I'm just playing a trick." The villagers were furious: "Don't shout wolf when there's no wolf!" And they walked back to the village.

3 The next day, Peter decided to play a trick again. "Wolf! Wolf! A wolf is attacking the sheep!" he shouted. The villagers arrived quickly. And they were furious again: "Don't tell lies!"

4 A week later, there was a real wolf. Peter shouted very loudly, "WOLF! WOLF!" But this time nobody rushed to help, and the wolf attacked the sheep.

1 **Look at the image. Circle the correct options. Use a dictionary to help you.**

The image shows a scene in [1] *a city / the country*. A boy is [2] *shouting / laughing* and there is a [3] *dog / sheep* next to him. We can also see a [4] *tiger / wolf*.

2 4.02 **Read and listen to the story. What is the moral? Check (✓) the correct answer.**

○ Don't shout. ○ Don't tell lies. ○ Don't attack the sheep.

3 **Read the story again. Answer the questions.**

1 How many people are there in Peter's family? Who are they?

Three. Peter, his dad, and his mom.

2 One day, Peter decides to shout "Wolf" when there is no wolf. Why?

....

3 Why do you think the villagers rush to help?

....

4 The villagers rush to help the second time Peter shouts "Wolf!," but not the third time. Why not?

....

5 How do you think Peter feels at the end of the story?

....

THINK!

In this story Peter has a second chance, but he doesn't have a third chance. Is it OK to give people a second chance when they tell lies? Is it OK to give them a third chance? Why / Why not?

WORKBOOK p.127

LANGUAGE IN CONTEXT

1 **Look at the examples below. Complete the sentences from the story.**

Simple Past of Regular Verbs: Affirmative	
I **liked** the story about Peter and the wolf.	
You **laughed** at Peter.	
He often [1] ________ his father on the farm.	
We **listened** to the story.	
The villagers [2] ________ to help.	
Most verbs	Add *–ed*, for example, play → **played**, walk → **walked**.
Verb ends in *–e*	Add *–d*, for example, arrive → **arrived**.
Verb ends in consonant + *–y*	Change *–y* to *–i* and add *–ed*, for example, try → **tried**.
Verb ends in consonant + vowel + consonant	Double the final consonant and add *–ed*, for example, plan → **planned**, stop → **stopped**.

LOOK!

Don't forget to include the *–d* at the end of the verb when you're talking about the past.

I like**d** the story.

2 **Write the simple past of the verbs. Check your answers in the story *Peter and the Wolf*.**

1 live ___lived___
2 decide ________
3 shout ________
4 arrive ________
5 ask ________
6 attack ________

3 **Complete the story. Use the simple past of the verbs.**

Mona [1] ___played___ (play) video games all day on the weekends. Her friend Lucy often [2] ________ (visit) her, but Mona never [3] ________ (open) the door. One Monday, Mona [4] ________ (decide) to stay home to play. She shouted, "Mom, I'm not well! Can I stay in bed?" "OK," her mother answered. Mona [5] ________ (rush) to her video game. Her mom was furious. The next day, the same thing happened. On the third day, Mona really wasn't well. Her mother [6] ________ (shout), "Don't tell lies! Go to school now." At school, Lucy [7] ________ (help) Mona a lot. She [8] ________ (walk) her home, too. Mona thanked Lucy, saying, "Thanks, you are a real friend."

USE IT!

4 **Complete sentences 1–4 so they are true for you using the correct form of the verbs.**

• ask • decide • help • live • visit • walk

1 In 2012 I ___lived in São Paulo.___
2 Last year I ________
3 Yesterday I ________
4 This morning I ________

5 **Talk to your partner about your sentences in Exercise 4.**

WORKBOOK p.124 and 126 PRACTICE EXTRA

LISTENING AND VOCABULARY

1 4.03 **Look at the image. Make predictions and answer the questions. Then listen and check.**

1 Where are the people?
 a in a library ◯
 b in a mall ◯
 c in a studio ◯
2 What are they doing?
 a asking and answering questions ◯
 b making a music album ◯
 c studying for an exam ◯

2 4.04 **Listen to the complete interview. Circle the correct options.**

1 Rosa talks about *clothes people like to wear* / *stories people talk about*.
2 Mystery Man is an example of *a radio show* / *an urban myth*.
3 *It is* / *It's not* possible to identify false stories on the Internet.

3 4.04 **Listen again and check (✓) the correct answer.**

1 John works …
 a at Radio Teen. ◯ b with Mystery Man. ◯ c in a restaurant. ◯
2 Mystery Man …
 a is real. ◯ b has red eyes. ◯ c likes photos. ◯
3 Rosa and John …
 a want more urban myths. ◯ b wear black pants. ◯ c know Mystery Man is fake. ◯

4 4.05 **Read the sentences and write *T* (true) or *F* (False). Then listen, check, and repeat the time expressions in bold.**

1 **One day**, John Green interviewed Rosa Lopez. ....
2 There weren't urban myths **in the past**. ....
3 **Years ago** people talked about urban myths at school. ....
4 People read and listen to urban myths online **now**. ....
5 Rosa Lopez read about Mystery Man **yesterday**. ....
6 There were false stories on the Internet **last week**. ....

WORKBOOK p.124 and 125

LANGUAGE IN CONTEXT

1 4.06 **Complete the simple past of the irregular verbs and the sentences from the interview in the charts. Use the words below. Then listen and check.**

• believe • read • saw • think

Irregular Verbs	
Infinitive	**Simple Past**
go	**went**
have	**had**
read	1 ______
say	**said**
see	2 ______
take	**took**

Simple Past: Negative
I 3 ______ the story.
You 4 ______ the story was true.
He **didn't write** the story.
We **didn't read** the book.
They **didn't post** the photos.

2 Complete the sentences with the correct simple past affirmative form of the verbs.

1 I __went__ (go) to Olinda on my last vacation.
2 My friends and I ______ (have) lunch at school yesterday.
3 Everybody in my class ______ (read) the post about Mystery Man.
4 Camila ______ (take) a lot of photos on her trip to Cancún.
5 I wanted a different book, so I ______ (say), "Let's go to the library!"

3 Put the words in parentheses in the correct order and complete the sentences.

1 I __didn't post stories__ (stories / post / didn't) about Mystery Man. I only posted true stories.
2 I ______ (movies / go / the / to / didn't) yesterday. I went on Saturday.
3 My friends and I ______ (this / story / didn't / read) last year. We read it last month.
4 My dad ______ (a / take / didn't / bus) to the hospital. He took a taxi.
5 You ______ (the / didn't / author / see) of the book, right? But I saw her.

USE IT!

4 Write sentences that are true for you about last weekend. Use the affirmative (+) or negative (–) form of the verbs in the charts in Exercise 1.

__I went horseback riding.__ __I didn't see my friends.__

1 (+) ______
2 (+) ______
3 (-) ______
4 (-) ______

5 Work in pairs. Take turns reading your sentences in Exercise 4. Then complete the chart with your partner's sentences. Start the sentences with your partner's name.

This is awesome ______
______

This is interesting ______
______

ACROSS THE CURRICULUM

HISTORY

The History of Storytelling

30,000 BC

A long time ago, people painted pictures on cave walls in different parts of the world. These visual stories included animals, people, and objects.

For many centuries, people didn't know how to write, and they listened to stories together. In Asia, people used paper puppets to tell stories.

More than 4,000 years ago

Sumerians used stones to tell the first written story in history.

15th century

Gutenberg from Germany invented the printing press. There were more books around, and more people learned to read. At this time, many people went to the theater, too.

The end of the 19th century

People started going to the movie theater.

1900–1970

People listened to stories on the radio and watched TV in their homes.

1970–1990s

A lot of new technologies arrived: video games, videocassettes, DVDs, and others.

1980–today

The Internet changed how we tell stories. Now we can watch movies and television online, and we can read other people's stories on social media. People tweet, blog, post, and share stories every day.

1 **Look at the timeline. Check (✓) the options to complete the sentence. Then read the text quickly to check your ideas.**

In the timeline, I think there is information about …

◯ clothes	◯ languages	◯ people
◯ dates	◯ objects	◯ places

2 4.07 **Read and listen to the text. Match 1–3 with a–c to make sentences about the text.**

1 The history of storytelling ....
2 There were many new ways to tell stories ....
3 New technologies help people ....

a in the 20th century.
b started a long time ago.
c tell stories in different ways.

WORDS IN CONTEXT

3 **Complete sentences 1–4 with the words below.**

• caves • share • storytelling • written

1 .... is the activity of writing or telling stories.
2 Is this an oral or a .... story?
3 In pre-history people lived in ....
4 I don't want it all for me. I want to .... it.

4 **Read the text again. Number the events in order 1–8.**

a cave paintings ...1...	d the Internet	g the television ....
b first written story	e the movie theater	h video games ....
c paper puppets	f the printing press	

5 **Circle the correct options.**

1 People in pre-history painted their stories in *different countries / one country*.
2 People used *paper / stones* to write the first written story in history.
3 The inventor of the printing press was from *Germany / Greece*.
4 There *were / weren't* theaters in the 15th century.
5 In the 19th century people *watched / didn't watch* movies at home.
6 People invented the videocassette and the Internet *in the same year / in different years*.

THINK!

In the past, people listened to stories with their friends and families. Now we watch movies and series alone. What is good about that? Is there anything bad?

WEBQUEST

Learn more! Check (✓) *True* or *False*.

There are prehistoric cave paintings in Piauí, Brazil.

◯ **True** ◯ **False**

VIDEO

4.2

1 **What is the video about?**
2 **Say two things that the actors can do.**

WRITING

www.alwaysfavoritestories.com

HOME COMEDY DRAMA **FANTASY** MYSTERY OTHERS

1 The Hobbit is a fantasy story by Tolkien. The main character is a hobbit named Bilbo. At the beginning, he lived a quiet life in Hobbiton.

2 One day, a wizard named Gandalf visited Bilbo. He asked Bilbo to go with him on an adventure with some dwarves. The dwarves wanted Bilbo to help them find their treasure.

3 At first, Bilbo didn't like the idea, but the adventure changed him. He went to many magical places and talked to unusual creatures.

4 At the end, there was a big battle. After that, Bilbo went back to his home and lived a quiet life again.

1 4.08 **Read and listen to the story summary. Match paragraphs 1–4 with descriptions a–d.**

a big, final event and conclusion ....

b details about how the main character reacts to the problem ....

c information about the title, author, and main character ....

d presentation of a problem that the main character has ....

2 **Match the time expressions (1–4) with the ideas they introduce in the text (a–d).**

1 At the beginning ....

2 One day ....

3 At first ....

4 At the end ....

a the main character's initial reaction to the problem

b the main character's situation when the story begins

c the main character's situation at the end of the story

d the problem the main character has

3 **Write a story summary.**

1 Choose a story you like.

2 Collect information about the title, author, main character, and sequence of actions.

3 Find or draw an image to illustrate the story.

4 Write the first version of your story summary.

4 **Switch your summary with a partner, and check his/her work. Use the checklist below.**

- ◯ title and author
- ◯ details about the main character
- ◯ clear sequence of actions
- ◯ time expressions
- ◯ verbs in the simple past

LOOK!

Sequence of Actions

Gandalf arrived at Bilbo's house. **Then** / **Next** he invited Bilbo to go on an adventure.

YOUR DIGITAL PORTFOLIO

Edit your summary, then publish it. Upload it to the class portfolio for everyone to see!

REVIEW
UNITS 3 AND 4

VOCABULARY

1 **Label the vacation activities (A–D). Then number the activities in your order of preference (1 = your favorite).**

A  ....

B  ....

C  ....

D  ....

2 **Look at the emojis in the messages. Complete the crossword puzzle.**

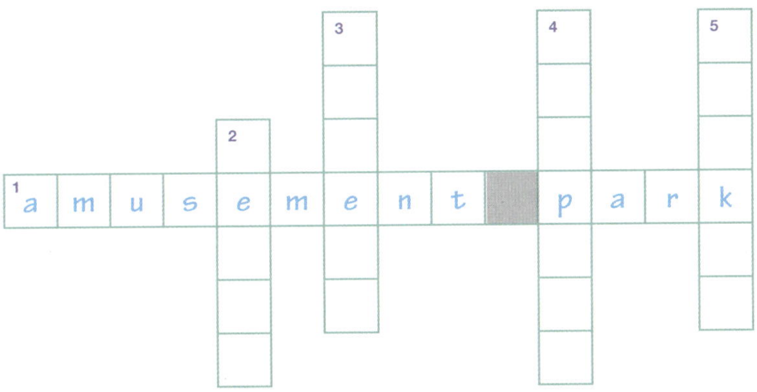

ACROSS →

1 Is there an [emoji] in your town?

DOWN ↓

2 I like the country, but I prefer the [emoji] .

3 There's a nice art [emoji] near here.

4 I always go [emoji] near here.

5 I love to visit a street [emoji] when I'm on vacation.

3 **Complete sentences 1–4. Use the words below. Then check (✓) the sentences that are true for you.**

• arrive • remember • rush • walk

1 I often .... out of the house on Monday mornings. ◯

2 I like to .... to the mall, but my sister prefers to take the bus. ◯

3 When I .... at school I often hang out with my friends at the athletic field. ◯

4 I think it's important to .... to drink a lot of water during the day. ◯

4 **Put the letters in the correct order to write time expressions. Then complete sentences a–d with the correct time expressions (1–4).**

1 ....in the past........ (ni het spta)

2 .... (alts ewke)

3 .... (sayre goa)

4 .... (noe yad)

a ....In the past........, people painted pictures to tell stories. We still like picture stories in the present.

b I lived near the beach when I was a child. .... my father said, "Let's go kayaking!"

c I didn't go to the street market .... I went there this week.

d .... , when my parents were teenagers, there was a farm here. Now there is a hotel.

LANGUAGE IN CONTEXT

5 Circle the correct options.

Nicolas Hey! How [1] (*was*) / *were* your weekend?

Paulina It [2] *was* / *were* great, thanks!

Nicolas [3] *Were you* / *You were* at the beach on Saturday morning?

Paulina No, I [4] *wasn't* / *weren't*. I was at the swimming pool.

Nicolas [5] *Was there* / *Were there* many people there?

Paulina No, not really. But [6] *there was* / *there were* a problem: the water was very cold.

Nicolas Oh, no!

6 Complete the conversation. Use the correct simple past form of the verbs.

Hi! I [1] ......arrived...... (arrive) here in Buenos Aires yesterday.

Cool! How are you?

Fine! I [2] .... (want) to stay at the hotel room playing video games last night, but my parents [3] .... (have) different plans …

Really?

Well, we [4] .... (go) to a restaurant, and after that we [5] .... (watch) a comedy show. I [6] .... (laugh) a lot!

😄😄

7 Look at what Rafael and Julia did on their vacations (✓). Then write sentences 1–4 using the correct affirmative or negative form of the simple past.

1 Rafael / go camping

....

2 Rafael / go kayaking

....

3 Julia / see the historic center

....

4 Rafael and Julia / visit a street market

....

CHECK YOUR PROGRESS

I CAN...

- talk about things to do on vacation 🙂 ◯ 🙁 ◯
- use the simple past of *to be* and *there was/were* 🙂 ◯ 🙁 ◯
- talk about stories and storytelling 🙂 ◯ 🙁 ◯
- use the simple past of regular and irregular verbs. 🙂 ◯ 🙁 ◯

LEARN TO LEARN

Finding examples of new words

Find examples of new words in different places, for example: on websites, in videos, in songs, in this book. Write the examples in your notebook. Read your examples often.

Example	Where from
1 Healthy foods we saw this year.	Blog www.foodblogforteens.com
2 They saw us at the park.	Actor in TV series "Always on Vacation"
3 But I saw her.	My English textbook, Unit 4

5 INCREDIBLE JOURNEYS

UNIT GOALS

- Talk about means of transportation.
- Read about an amazing traveler.
- Listen to a radio show.
- Learn about transportation in Hong Kong.
- Interview someone about how they traveled to school in the past.

THINK!

1 Look at the photo. What can you see?

2 How was traveling different 100 years ago?

VIDEO 4.1

1 How did Ancient Egyptians travel on the River Nile?

2 What famous things did they build?

VOCABULARY IN CONTEXT

TRANSPORTATION

1 5.01 **Read the facts about everyday journeys and write the means of transportation. Then listen, check, and repeat.**

- airplane
- boat
- car
- ferry
- motorcycle
- scooter
- ~~subway~~
- taxi
- van

/// EVERYDAY JOURNEYS ///

Metro, the [1] subway system in São Paulo, takes 5.2 million passengers every day.

The Airbus A380 is an enormous [2] .... It can take 850 passengers!

The electric [3] .... is popular for short trips in cities.

People all over the world get to work and school by [4] .... In China, there are almost 200 million!

In Brazil and many other countries, millions of children use a [5] .... to get to school.

In Giethoorn in the Netherlands, there aren't roads. You can travel by [6] ....

You can take a [7] .... anytime on the streets of New York. There are 13,587 yellow cars.

Many families travel by [8] .... in Thailand. There are around 20 million in the country.

Can you get from Europe to Asia in 20 minutes? Yes! Take a [9] .... across the Bosphorus strait in Istanbul, Turkey.

2 5.02 **Listen and match situations 1–5 with the means of transportation a–e.**

a airplane ....
b bike 1
c ferry ....
d subway ....
e taxi ....

3 **Write the means of transportation the people are about to use. Use the words below.**

• bike • boat • ~~bus~~ • car • motorcycle • train

1

bus

2

3

4

5

6

4 **Write the means of transportation in Exercises 1–3 in the chart. Then write two more words in each column. Use a dictionary to help you.**

Land	Air	Water
car		

USE IT!

5 **Complete the chart with your answers.**

	My Answers	My Classmate's Answers
1 Means of transportation you use every week		
2 How you get to school		
3 How you get to the grocery store		
4 Favorite car color		
5 Means of transportation you like to use		
6 Means of transportation you never use		

6 **Work in pairs. Take turns to share your information from Exercise 5. Write your classmate's answers in the chart.**

The means of transportation I use every week is a bike. What about you?

I use the bus.

READING

AMAZING TRAVELERS

Fact sheet #22 – Nellie Bly (1864–1922)

Who was Nellie Bly?
She was an American journalist. She traveled around the world in 72 days in 1889–1890.

What was the inspiration for her journey?
Jules Verne's book *Around the World in Eighty Days*.

Where did she grow up?
She grew up in Pennsylvania. Her family was poor. Her father died when she was six.

How did she become a journalist?
When Bly was 18, she wrote a letter to a newspaper. The editor liked her letter and offered her a job. In 1887, she started to work for a famous newspaper, the *New York World*.

When did she start her journey?
On November 14, 1889, at 9:40 a.m. Bly left New Jersey on a ship to England – the first of many ships on her journey.

When did she arrive back?
On January 25, 1890. Her journey took 72 days, 6 hours, 11 minutes, and 14 seconds. It was a world record!

Did you know?
- The *New York World* made a board game about her journey.
- She took only one suitcase!

1 **Look at the fact sheet. Write *T* (true) or *F* (false).**

The fact sheet …

1 is biographical. ....
2 is organized into long paragraphs. ....
3 is organized into questions and answers. ....
4 has images. ....

2 5.03 **Read and listen to the fact sheet. Then complete sentences 1–6 with the words below. There are six extra words.**

- board game
- book
- England
- father
- mother
- movie
- newspaper
- ship
- train
- ~~the United States~~
- 1864
- 1887

1 Nellie Bly was a journalist from *the United States*.
2 The inspiration for her journey was a ....
3 Her .... died when she was a child.
4 She started to work for the *New York World* in ....
5 To start her journey, Bly traveled by .... to England.
6 In the 19th century, there was a .... about her journey.

3 **Read the fact sheet again. Match information a–f with facts 1–6.**

a 1864 *4*
b 72 ....
c 80 ....
d November 14, 1889 ....
e January 25, 1890 ....
f 1 ....

1 number of days of an around-the-world journey in Jules Verne's book
2 number of suitcases Nellie Bly took on her journey
3 date Nellie Bly finished her trip
4 year Nellie Bly was born
5 number of days of Nellie Bly's around-the-world journey
6 date Nellie Bly started her trip

THINK!

Imagine you are Nellie Bly. You can take only one small suitcase on your around-the-world journey. What do you pack?

WORKBOOK p.131

LANGUAGE IN CONTEXT

1 **Look at the examples below. Complete the sentences from the fact sheet.**

Simple Past of Regular and Irregular Verbs: Questions and Answers

***Yes/No* Questions (?)**	**Short Answers**
Did I **write** about Nellie Bly?	Yes, I **did**. / No, I **didn't**.
Did you **know** she was a journalist?	Yes, you **did**. / No, you **didn't**.
Did she **travel** by train?	Yes, she **did**. / No, she **didn't**.
Did we **read** the newspaper?	Yes, we **did**. / No, we **didn't**.
Did they **like** Bly's story?	Yes, they **did**. / No, they **didn't**.
***Wh–* Questions (?)**	**Answers**
Where [1] .... she .... up?	In Pennsylvania.
How [2] .... she .... a journalist?	She wrote a letter to a newspaper.
When [3] .... she .... her journey?	On November 14, 1889.

2 **Write *Yes/No* Questions.**

1 ....Did.... you ....go.... to the movies last night? (go)
2 .... Mark .... the movie with you? (watch)
3 .... the students .... Nellie Bly's biography? (read)
4 .... Nellie Bly .... to Brazil? (come)

LOOK!

Use the infinitive form of the verb in questions.

Did you **go** to school by bus?

3 **Look at the list of things Nellie Bly took on her journey. Write questions.**

1 Nellie Bly / take / a big suitcase / ?
....Did Nellie Bly take a big suitcase?....
2 How many / hats / have / in her suitcase / ?
....
3 she / put / slippers / in her suitcase / ?
....
4 What / she / use / to carry water / ?
....
5 How / she / write / during her journey / ?
....

a small suitcase

two hats

a flask and a cup

slippers

paper, pen, and ink

4 **Write the answers to questions 1–5 in Exercise 3 in your notebook.**

....1 No, she didn't. She took a small suitcase....

USE IT!

5 **Work in pairs. Ask and answer questions 1–4 about a real or imaginary journey.**

1 Where / you / go / ?
2 How / you / get / there / ?
3 What / you / see / ?
4 What / you / take / ?

Where did you go?

WORKBOOK p.128 and 130 PRACTICE EXTRA

LISTENING AND VOCABULARY

1 5.04 **Complete actions 1–7 with the verbs below. Then listen, check, and repeat.**

• ~~board~~ • drive • get (x 2) • miss • ride • take • wait

1 b o a r d an airplane

2 g_____ **on** / t_____ the train

3 g_____ **off** the train

4 m_____ the bus

5 w_____ **for** the bus

6 d_____ a car

7 r_____ a bike

2 **Look at the two cities on the map. Can you guess how long the journey between them took in the 1920s?**

- ◯ 11–14 hours
- ◯ 8–10 days
- ◯ 2–3 months

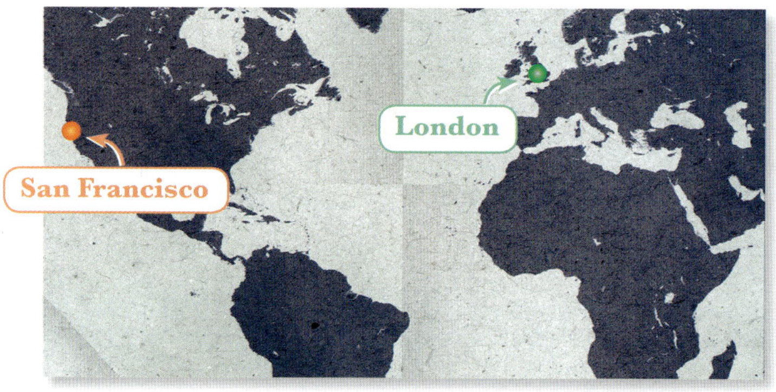

3 5.05 **Listen to the radio show. Was your guess in Exercise 2 correct? Which five means of transportation do the presenters mention?**

1 airplane
2 ______
3 ______
4 ______
5 ______

4 5.05 **Listen again. Write *T* (true) or *F* (false).**

In the 1920s, ...

1 it was difficult to travel. T
2 cars were very popular. ______
3 people planned their journeys. ______
4 people often traveled by airplane. ______
5 a journey across the Atlantic took several days. ______
6 people took buses from Southampton to London. ______

WORKBOOK p.128 and 129

LANGUAGE IN CONTEXT

1 **Complete the sentences from the radio show in the chart. Use *could* or *couldn't*.**

***Could* for Ability in the Past**					
Affirmative (+)			**Negative (–)**		
I / You / He / She / It / We / They	1	**take** around ten days.	I / You / He / She / It / We / They	2	**travel** quickly.
***Yes/No* Questions (?)**			**Short Answers**		
Could	I / you / he / she / it /we / they	**travel** by airplane?	Yes, / No,	I / you / he / she / it / we / they	**could** / **couldn't**.

2 **Complete the sentences with *could* or *couldn't*.**

1 I ..couldn't.. dance well when I was five. (–)
2 My cousins .... drive a car when they were 19. (+)
3 My teacher .... speak English in high school. (+)
4 Laura .... take the bus to school last year. (+)
5 The students .... read fast. (–)
6 We .... do our homework. It was difficult. (–)

3 **Write questions for an interview in your notebook. Use *can* or *could* and the ideas in 1–6.**

Now	1 go to the movie theater alone ◯ 	2 take a bus alone ◯ 	3 swim ◯ 
Five years ago	4 play volleyball ◯ 	5 ride a bike ◯ 	6 read long books ◯ 

1 Can you go to the movie theater alone now?

USE IT!

4 **Work in pairs. Take turns asking and answering the questions in Exercise 3. Check (✓) or (x) the images for your partner.**

5 **Work with a different partner. Take turns sharing your classmate's answers from Exercise 4.**

Gabriela can go to the movie theater alone.

Rafael couldn't ride a bike five years ago.

WORKBOOK p.128 and 130 PRACTICE EXTRA

AROUND THE WORLD

www.travelwithtom.myblog

ABOUT ME TRAVEL TIPS POSTS REVIEWS CONTACT ME

June 21

GETTING AROUND ... HONG KONG WITH TOM!

Hong Kong Island is a fantastic place, with almost eight million inhabitants. But it's easy for tourists to use public transportation! I could visit all the places in the city during my week there.

Getting around score: ★★★★★

Transportation in Hong Kong

1 The Mass Transit Railway (MTR) is a very popular transportation system. It combines **subway**, **trains**, and **trams**.

Some trams have two decks, like buses in London

A tram going to Victoria Peak

2 A tram takes people to Victoria Peak, a famous mountain. The tram started to operate in 1888.

3 Cars drive on the left, like in the United Kingdom. I couldn't drive there, but that was OK.

People using a moving walkway

4 Escalators and moving walkways connect one part of the city to another, high on the mountain.

5 You can't eat or drink on the MTR trains or in the stations.

Red taxis

6 Taxis from different areas of the island are different colors – red, green, and blue.

7 You can get from Hong Kong to China by train, plane, or car, but many people prefer to take the ferry. I took the ferry across the harbor to Shenzhen and had a great time.

↓ Comments 25

Buy tickets for the ferry to Shenzhen!

1 **Look at the review of Hong Kong. Circle the correct options.**

1 The review presents interesting information about *public transportation / activities* in Hong Kong.

2 Tom wrote the review for *Hongkongers / visitors*.

2 **What elements show the text is a review?**

◯ star rating ◯ comments ◯ link to buy tickets

3 5.06 **Read and listen to the blog review. Match items 1–7 in the review with questions a–g.**

Which item …

a is about food and drink on public transportation? 5

b mentions similarities between Hong Kong and the United Kingdom? ....

c is about two unusual means of transportation? ....

d mentions colors as a way to organize public transportation? ....

e mentions a means of transportation from the 19th century? ....

f mentions how people can travel from Hong Kong to another territory? ....

g is about a combination of means of transportation? ....

4 **Read the review again. Answer the questions.**

1 How many people live in Hong Kong?

Almost eight million people.

2 What is the score for public transportation in Hong Kong?

....

3 What means of transportation can you use to visit Victoria Peak?

....

4 What can't you do on the MTR trains?

....

5 What is a popular means of transportation between Hong Kong and China?

....

WORDS IN CONTEXT

5 **Match 1–4 with A–D.**

1 escalator ....

2 harbor ....

3 mountain ....

4 railway ....

A

B

C

D

THINK!

Imagine you are a tourist in Hong Kong. What other information about transportation do you need?

WEBQUEST

Learn more! Check (✓) the correct answer.

In the past, junks were a popular means of transportation in Hong Kong, but now they are for tourists only. Junks are …

◯ **cars.** ◯ **boats.** ◯ **trams.**

VIDEO

3.2

1 Why is traffic a problem?

2 Which countries are in the video?

SPEAKING

ASKING QUESTIONS ABOUT THE PAST

1 5.07 **Read and listen to Luisa asking her uncle some questions. What two means of transportation do they talk about?**

Luisa	**Uncle Jake**, can I ask you some questions?
Uncle Jake	Sure!
Luisa	How did you get to school when you were ten years old?
Uncle Jake	I **took the school bus**.
Luisa	Interesting … Was the journey long?
Uncle Jake	**No, it wasn't**.
Luisa	Did you ever **ride a bike** to school?
Uncle Jake	**No, I didn't**. I **couldn't ride a bike.**
Luisa	OK. Thank you.

LIVING ENGLISH

2 Read the dialogue in Exercise 1 again. Write the correct expressions.

What do you say when you want to …

1 check if you can ask questions?

....

2 agree with something?

....

3 show interest in a conversation?

....

3 5.08 **Listen, check, and repeat the expressions.**

PRONUNCIATION

4 5.09 **Listen to sentences 1–3 about Luisa's uncle. Pay attention to the pronunciation of *–ed* in the simple past.**

1 He <u>worked</u> for a newspaper. He <u>liked</u> his job.

2 He <u>started</u> his journey in March. He <u>boarded</u> a ship.

3 He <u>traveled</u> to China. He <u>arrived</u> in May.

5 5.09 **Listen again and repeat.**

6 5.07 **Listen to the dialogue again. Then practice with a partner.**

7 Role play a new dialogue. Follow the steps.

1 Interview your partner about how they traveled to school when they were ten years old.

2 Change the words in **blue** in Exercise 1 to write a new dialogue in your notebook.

3 Practice your dialogue with a partner.

4 Present your dialogue to the class.

YOUR DIGITAL PORTFOLIO

Record your interview and upload it to your class digital portfolio.

PRACTICE EXTRA

6

HEROES MAKE A DIFFERENCE

UNIT GOALS

- Talk about personality and feelings.
- Read about an everyday hero.
- Listen to an interview.
- Learn about the Olympic Games.
- Write a social media post.

THINK!

1 Do you think firefighters are heroes? Why?
2 What kind of person can be a hero?

VIDEO

5.1

1 Say two famous heroes in the video.
2 Where is Yash Gupta from?

VOCABULARY IN CONTEXT

PERSONALITY ADJECTIVES

1 6.01 **Complete the title of the fact file and write labels for the athletes with the words below. Then listen, check, and repeat.**

• ~~amazing~~ • boring • brave • smart • friendly • funny • kind • lazy • strong

1 AMAZING PEOPLE

A

Serena Williams can speak English, Spanish, French, and some Italian.

2 ________

Wow! Gold medal in the 2012 Olympics.

B

Sérgio Santos (Serginho) loves to talk to his fans.

3 ________

Wow! Volleyball Olympic Champion in 2004 and 2016.

C

Usain Bolt did a special pose when he won a race.

4 ________

NOT 5 ________

Wow! Olympic gold in 100m and 200m in three Olympic Games.

D

Carissa Moore is a surfer. She surfs most days and she wins lots of competitions.

6 ________

NOT 7 ________

Wow! First athlete to win a Triple Crown Event at age 16.

E

Henry Wanyoike helps other people with eye problems in Kenya.

8 ________

Wow! First African to win a Paralympic gold medal (5000m in Sydney 2000).

F

Yusra Mardini's boat had an accident and she helped save the other people.

9 ________

Wow! Yusra left Syria by boat in 2015 because of the war. She was in the first Refugee Olympic team in Rio 2016.

2 **Match 1–9 with a–i.**

1 Sara only talks about swimming. a
2 Roger Federer often talks to his fans before practice. ____
3 Beatriz Ferreira is a world boxing champion. ____
4 My cousin is an athlete. He wakes up at 4 a.m. every day to practice. ____
5 Serena Williams speaks a lot of languages. ____
6 Yusra Mardini shares her stories on social media to help other refugees. ____
7 Shaquille O'Neal's posts on social media always make me laugh. ____
8 Michael Phelps has 28 Olympic medals. ____
9 Marta left her family when she was 14 to play professional soccer. ____

a She's really **boring**.
b He's not **lazy**.
c He's so **funny**!
d He is really **amazing**!
e He's very **friendly**.
f She's really **kind**!
g She's very **smart**.
h She's really **strong**.
i She's very **brave**.

3 **Complete the chart with the words in bold in Exercise 2.**

How often do these words describe you?		
Always	**Sometimes**	**Never**

USE IT!

4 **Write sentences about you and four other people. Use the words in bold in Exercise 2 and *always*, *sometimes*, or *never*.**

1 I ____
2 My best friend ____
3 (a member of your family) My ____
4 (a teacher) My ____
5 (a celebrity) ____

5 **Work in pairs. Read your sentences in Exercise 4 to your partner. Make comments about your classmate's sentences.**

I'm funny. I always make my friends laugh.

I know!

I agree.

No way!

Really!?

Yeah.

READING

www.newsforyoungpeople.online

HOME
MOVIES
GAMES
PEOPLE
PLACES
SPORTS
APPS

CAN WE SEE WITH OUR EARS?

A

B

Daniel Kish can't see: he went blind when he was a baby, but he learned to use sound to become more independent.

When he was a teenager Daniel wanted to ride a bike like his friends. He decided to learn by riding next to a wall. Soon he was riding his bike to school.

One day, a smart friend was watching Daniel. He noticed something amazing: Daniel wasn't using his eyes to see, he was making clicking sounds and using his ears to "see" objects around him.

Dolphins make similar sounds to locate fish: the sound travels through the air until it hits a fish. The sound bounces off the fish and returns to the dolphin. **This technique is called echolocation, and bats also use it.** Using echolocation, Daniel knows the size and position of an object so he can "see" it in his head.

C

Now, Daniel travels around the world talking about echolocation. He believes anyone can use the technique! Daniel helps other blind people to learn so they can enjoy activities such as cycling, camping, and cooking, just like he does. He is an everyday hero!

1 Look at the text. Then circle the correct options.

The text is *a biography / an article* about *a smart and kind person / an amazing athlete*.

2 Match the blue sentences in the text with images A–C.

3 6.02 Read and listen to the text. Number these details in order 1–4.

a What echolocation is and how it works ....

b What Daniel's friend saw when he rode his bike ....

c How Daniel learned to use echolocation ....

d What Daniel does now and what he thinks ....

4 Read the text again. Write *T* (true) or *F* (false). Then correct the false sentences.

1 When Daniel Kish was born he couldn't see. F

He went blind when he was a baby.

2 Daniel makes clicking sounds when he wants to "see" something. ....

....

3 Daniel doesn't like to teach other people how to use echolocation. ....

....

4 Blind people can use echolocation to talk to animals. ....

....

THINK!

Why is Daniel an everyday hero? Do you agree with this description? Why / Why not? What can you do to be an everyday hero?

WORKBOOK p.135

LANGUAGE IN CONTEXT

1 **Look at the examples below. Complete the sentences from the article.**

Past Progressive	
Affirmative (+)	**Negative (–)**
I **was using** clicking sounds. You **were using** your ears to "see". He [1]........................ his bike to school. We **were riding** our bikes to school. They **were learning** about echolocation.	I **wasn't looking** at the objects. You **weren't talking** about bats. Daniel [2]........................ his eyes. We **weren't taking** the bus to school. They **weren't having** a science class.

2 **Look at the image. What were the people doing last Saturday? Write sentences using the past progressive form of the verbs below.**

eat • get • ~~listen~~ • read • ride • use

> **LOOK!**
> **We don't use contractions in the affirmative form of the past progressive.**
> On Thursday he **was** wearing jeans.

1 Andre ......was listening to music......
2 Bruna and Juan ....
3 Felipe ....
4 Laura ....
5 Ryan ....
6 Gisela ....

3 **Complete the sentences with the past progressive negative form of the verbs.**

1 You ......weren't wearing...... (wear) a blue sweatshirt yesterday.
2 The teachers .... (talk) to the students.
3 The dolphin .... (sing).
4 Abigail .... (read) about bats.

USE IT!

4 **Complete the sentences with the past progressive so they are true for you. Then tell your partner.**

1 I .... at 6 a.m. yesterday.
2 I .... at 4 p.m. last Saturday.
3 At this time a week ago I ....

WORKBOOK p.132 and 133 PRACTICE EXTRA

LISTENING AND VOCABULARY

1 6.03 **Label images 1–8 with the words below. Then listen, check, and repeat. How is the superhero avatar feeling?**

- angry
- bored
- excited
- ~~happy~~
- sad
- surprised
- tired
- worried

Feelings

1 happy
2 ....
3 ....
4 ....
5 ....
6 ....
7 ....
8 ....

2 6.04 **Listen to an interview with Bruno and check (✓) the correct option.**

In the interview Bruno tells a story about a day when …

a he met a superhero. ◯
b he did something amazing. ◯
c he was on vacation. ◯

3 6.04 **Which three words did you hear in the interview? Listen and check.**

◯ sad ◯ tired ◯ bored ◯ surprised ◯ worried ◯ angry

4 6.04 **Listen again and number the events in order 1–7.**

1 a Bruno was walking to school.
.... b He called an ambulance.
.... c He arrived at school.
.... d He shouted for help.
.... e He was late.
.... f He saw a man in the middle of the road.
.... g A woman helped.

5 **Complete the sentences with the words below.**

- amazing
- ~~angry~~
- boring
- happy
- tired
- worried

1 Bruno's teacher was angry because Bruno was late for school.
2 Bruno was .... because it was a Monday morning.
3 Bruno was .... because the man wasn't moving.
4 The interviewer was .... to know that the man was OK.
5 The teenager's actions were .... because he saved a man's life.
6 At the end of the day, Bruno thought, "It wasn't a .... Monday."

WORKBOOK p.132 and 133

LANGUAGE IN CONTEXT

1 **Complete the questions and answers from the interview in the chart. Use *was/were*.**

Past Progressive: Questions and Answers

***Yes/No* Questions (?)**	**Short Answers**	
Was I **saving** a man's life?	Yes, I [1]	No, I **wasn't**.
[2] .... you **walking** to school?	Yes, you **were**.	No, you **weren't**.
Was he/she **lying down** in the street?	Yes, he/she **was**.	No, he/she **wasn't**.
Were we **listening** to the right show?	Yes, we **were**.	No, we **weren't**.
Were they **talking** to a 13-year-old?	Yes, they **were**.	No, they **weren't**.
***Wh–* Questions (?)**	**Answers**	
What [3] .... he **doing**?	He wasn't moving.	
How was Bruno **feeling**?	He was so worried.	
Where were Bruno and the woman **helping** the man?	In the middle of the street.	

2 **Complete the mini dialogues. Use the correct affirmative or negative form of *was/were*.**

1 **A** .... you talking to your teachers yesterday afternoon? **B** Yes, I ....

2 **A** .... the man moving? **B** No, he ....

3 **A** .... you and Liam helping Sarah last night? **B** Yes, we ....

4 **A** .... Bruno and the woman laughing? **B** No, they ....

3 **Put the words in the correct order to make questions. Then match questions 1–4 with answers a–d.**

1 was / interview / in / the / why / the / laughing / athlete / ? ....d.....
.................Why was the athlete laughing in the interview?.................

2 going / were / they / where / ? ....
....

3 man / what / saying / the / was / ? ....
....

4 was / who / the / helping / children / ? ....
....

a To the stadium.
b Their teachers.
c That he was very worried.
d Because the reporter was very funny.

USE IT!

4 **Work in pairs. Think about what you were doing at these times yesterday: 8 a.m., 1 p.m., 9 p.m. Take turns doing actions, and asking and answering. Change the words in blue.**

At 9 p.m. were you doing your homework?

No, I wasn't.

Were you playing the piano?

Yes, I was!

WORKBOOK p.132 and 134 PRACTICE EXTRA

ACROSS THE CURRICULUM

PHYSICAL EDUCATION

THE OLYMPIC GAMES: A SHORT HISTORY

Origins

The Olympic Games started in **Olympia, Greece** about 3,000 years ago. There were games every four years in the summer until the Roman Emperor Theodosius prohibited them in the 4th century A.D. The Olympic athletes were great heroes to the Greek people.

Modern games

The first modern Olympic Games were in Athens in 1896, but women couldn't participate until Paris 1900. There are Summer and Winter Olympic Games every four years. The first **Paralympic Games** were in Rome, Italy, in 1960. Olympic athletes work a lot and inspire other people.

A

....

B

....

C

....

D

....

Some Sports Events in Ancient Greece

- **Discus and javelin:** similar to sports events with the same name in modern times.
- Long jump: athletes had weights called halteres when they jumped.
- Equestrian sports: horse races and chariot races.

Fun Facts

- Winners didn't get medals. The prize was **a crown of leaves**.
- People didn't take note of time or distance results.
- Athletes didn't wear clothes during competitions.
- Women couldn't compete, and only unmarried women could watch a sports event.

1 **Look at the fact file. Label images A–D with the phrases in blue.**

2 6.05 **Read and listen to the fact file. Check (✓) the sentences that are true for you.**

1 The images helped me understand the text. ○
2 It contains some information I knew before reading. ○
3 I learned something new. ○
4 There was something funny. ○
5 I was surprised by something. ○

WORDS IN CONTEXT

3 **Match the phrases in bold (1–4) with the words and phrases (a–d).**

1 The athletes trained **from the beginning to the end of** the night. ....
2 In the ancient Olympics people used a **vehicle with two horses**. ....
3 Women couldn't **compete** in the games at first. ....
4 The winners get a **valuable thing**. ....

a prize
b chariot
c during
d participate in a race or competition

4 **Complete the diagram with the phrases below.**

• crown of leaves • discus throwing • female athletes • medals for winners • summer games

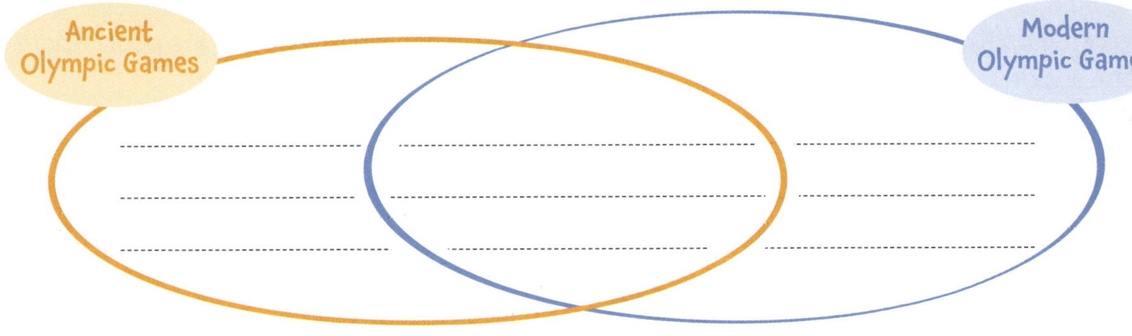

5 **Match images 1–5 with actions a–e. What sport from the fact file do the images show?**

1

2

3

4

5

a Jump: with arms up. ....
b Finish jump: throw halteres down. ....
c Prepare for jump: move arms. ....
d In the air: move arms to the front. ....
e Start: hold halteres down. 1

THINK!

The Olympic athletes were great heroes to the Greek people. Do you think modern athletes are great heroes? Why / Why not?

WEBQUEST

Learn more! Check (✓) the correct answer.

Young athletes (aged 15–18) can compete in the Youth Olympic Games. How often do these games happen?

○ **every 2 years** ○ **every 3 years** ○ **every 4 years**

VIDEO

1.2

1 Say two things superheroes can do.
2 What famous poet is in the video?

WRITING

Everyday heroes | Matt Smith | Home | Create | Group info | ?

Everyday heroes

23 participants

About

Discussion

Members

Events

Photos

Matt Smith

1 day ago

My soccer coach is a hero to me. I can tell a lot of stories about her, but what she did at our game last weekend was very special. We were winning the game 1–0. The other team wasn't playing badly, but we were playing really well. At the end of the game, the result was 3–0, and I could see that one of their players was really sad. We were celebrating our victory, but Coach Laura walked toward that player. She said to him, "Don't be sad, you played very well, there's always the next match." He looked at her and smiled. Isn't she a hero? #everydayheroes

1 Look at the post. Check (✓) the correct answers.

1 Who wrote the post?
- a Coach Laura ◯
- b Matt Smith ◯

2 Where can we read the post?
- a on a social media group ◯
- b on the author's blog ◯

3 How can we respond to the post? There is more than one possible answer.
- a recording an audio ◯
- b sharing the post ◯
- c writing a comment ◯

2 6.06 Read and listen to the post. Match 1–5 with a–e.

1 The first sentence ...c...

2 The second sentence ......

3 "We were winning the game 1–0." ......

4 The question "Isn't she a hero?" ......

5 The hashtag (#) "everydayheroes" ......

a introduces a specific event.

b helps readers to find other posts about everyday heroes.

c introduces the person the author is writing about.

d invites the reader to respond to the post.

e gives details about a specific event.

3 Write a social media post about a personal hero.

1 Choose a person to write about.

2 Collect information about the person.

3 Find or draw an image of the person to illustrate your post.

4 Write the first version of your post. Use vocabulary from the unit.

4 Switch your post with a partner, and check his/her work. Use the checklist below.

◯ details about the person

◯ clear sequence of ideas

◯ verbs in the past progressive

LOOK!

We use different words to refer to people.

My soccer coach is a hero to me. I can tell a lot of stories about **her**.

YOUR DIGITAL PORTFOLIO

Edit your post, then publish it. Upload it to the class portfolio for everyone to see!

REVIEW
UNITS 5 AND 6

VOCABULARY

1 Label the images with the correct means of transportation.

1 

2 

3 

4 

s..................... m.............................. s................ a.......................

2 Complete the sentences. Use the verbs below.

• board • drive • miss • take

1 Did you .... the school van again, Marco? You're always late for class!
2 My dad didn't .... the subway to work yesterday.
3 The passengers are waiting to .... the airplane.
4 My sister can .... , but she never takes me to school.

3 Circle the correct options.

1 We always laugh at Isabela's stories. She's very *smart* / *funny*.
2 My cousin often helps me with my homework. She's *kind* / *lazy*.
3 Marcelo talks about video games all the time. He's *boring* / *brave*.
4 Charlotte speaks English, Spanish, and French. She's *smart* / *strong*.

4 Match the people in bold with the way they are feeling (a–d).

1 **Nick** went to bed at 1 a.m. and got up at 6 a.m. ....
2 The students in **Mr. Brown**'s class are always late. ....
3 **Juana** is waiting for the bus. She doesn't have a cell phone or a book. ....
4 **Haruto**'s mom made a chocolate cake for him, but it's not his birthday. ....

a angry
b bored
c surprised
d tired

LANGUAGE IN CONTEXT

5 Put the words in the correct order to write questions.

1 travel / Mariko / did / airplane / by / last year / ?
Did Mariko travel by airplane last year?
2 the students / the van / yesterday / what time / did / take / ?
....
3 Mary and Jane / for an hour / the bus / did / wait for / before school / ?
....
4 miss / did / Jake / why / the train / this morning / ?
....

6 **Look at the chart about what two teenagers could and couldn't do when they were six years old. Write questions and answers.**

	ride a bike	read books
Liam	✓	×
Camila	×	✓

Liam

1 .... Could Liam ride a bike? ....

.... Yes, he could. ....

2 ....

....

Camila

3 ....

....

4 ....

....

7 **Complete the text with the affirmative or negative forms of the past progressive.**

This morning, at 9 a.m. the 7th grade students [1] ...... were taking ...... (take) a science test, but they [2] .... (not do) the test in their classroom. They were in the science lab. Mr. White [3] .... (not correct) homework. He [4] .... (teach) an English class. The school van driver [5] .... (not arrive) at school. She [6] .... (leave) school.

8 **Look at the images of the park yesterday. Complete the questions with the past progressive form of the verbs. Then answer the questions.**

1

...... Were ...... Jen, Bob and Tom ...... using ...... (use) their cell phones?

Yes, ... they were ......

2

What .... the Garcias .... (do)?

....

3

What .... Marissa .... (do)?

....

4

.... the teenagers .... (have) a picnic?

....

CHECK YOUR PROGRESS

I CAN...

- talk about means of transportation
- use simple past questions and *could/couldn't*
- talk about personality and feelings
- use the past progressive.

LEARN TO LEARN

Drawing

Draw simple images in your notebook to help you remember vocabulary.

7 GREAT IDEAS

UNIT GOALS

- Talk about famous firsts and technology.
- Read about teen inventors.
- Listen to a game show.
- Learn about technology in Estonia.
- Tell an anecdote.

THINK!

1 Look at the photo. What are they doing?

2 How can we help each other have great ideas?

VIDEO

7.1

1 What were movies like in 1926?

2 What did John Logie Baird do?

VOCABULARY IN CONTEXT

INNOVATION VERBS

1 7.01 **Read the quiz about famous firsts. Complete the questions with the words below. Then listen, chec and repeat.**

- become
- build
- ~~create~~
- discover
- fly
- invent
- start
- take
- use

FAMOUS FIRSTS

When did ...

1 Ada Lovelace ...create... the first computer algorithm with Charles Babbage?

2 Alexander Fleming .... penicillin, the first antibiotic?

3 Maria Telkes and Eleanor Raymond .... the first house heated with solar energy?

4 Hattie McDaniel .... the first African American to get an Oscar?

5 Joseph Nicéphore Niépce .... the first photograph with a camera?

6 people .... to send text messages via WhatsApp?

7 Josephine Cochrane .... the first dishwasher?

8 Amelia Earhart .... across the Atlantic Ocean for the first time?

9 Pixar first .... computers to make an animated movie?

2 **Write the simple past forms of the verbs in Exercise 1 in the chart. Use the irregular verb list on page 110 to help you.**

Regular Verbs	Irregular Verbs
created	

3 **Write the correct simple past verbs from the chart in Exercise 2 in sentences 1–9.**

1 Ada Lovelace created the first computer algorithm with Charles Babbage in the *19th century* / *20th century*.
2 Alexander Fleming .... penicillin, the first antibiotic, in *1807* / *1928*.
3 Maria Telkes and Eleanor Raymond .... the first house heated with solar energy in *1948* / *1998*.
4 Hattie McDaniel .... the first African American to get an Oscar in *1909* / *1940*.
5 Joseph Nicéphore Niépce .... the first photograph with a camera in the *1820s* / *1920s*.
6 People .... to send text messages via WhatsApp in *1999* / *2009*.
7 Josephine Cochrane .... the first dishwasher in *1886* / *1986*.
8 Amelia Earhart .... across the Atlantic Ocean for the first time in *1902* / *1932*.
9 Pixar first .... computers to make an animated movie in *1985* / *1995*.

4 7.02 **Circle the correct dates in Exercise 3 to complete the answers to the quiz. Then listen and check.**

5 **Work in pairs. Match 1–6 with a–f to make questions.**

1 When did Marta Vieira da Silva b
2 When did Beyoncé ....
3 When did scientists ....
4 When did the Brazilian government ....
5 When did Emerson Fittipaldi ....

a discover prehistoric cave paintings in Mato Grosso do Sul?
b start to play soccer for Brazil?
c build Brasília?
d become the first Brazilian to win the Formula One World Championship?
e create her first perfume?

USE IT!

6 **Work in pairs. Take turns asking the questions in Exercise 5 and guessing the dates.**

- from 1956 to 1960
- in 1972
- in 2002
- in 2009 (x 2)

When did Marta Vieira da Silva start to play soccer for Brazil?

I think she started to play for Brazil in 2009.

READING

TEEN INVENTORS

By Clara Silva, August 20

Ann Makosinski

- Born in 1997
- Student and inventor
- Lives in Victoria, Canada
- Invention: a flashlight that uses body heat to create light

Shubham Banerjee

- Born in 2001
- Student and inventor
- Lives in Santa Clara, the United States
- Invention: a cheap Braille printer

Ann Makosinski always liked building things. As a young teenager, she was studying electronics while her friends were playing video games.
Ann was visiting her mother's family in the Philippines when she had the idea for the flashlight. Her inspiration? A friend that was having problems at school because she didn't have light to study at night.
In 2013, her invention won the Google Science Fair for 15–16-year-olds.

Shubham Banerjee was a curious child. He loved science and participated in science fairs at his elementary school.
He built the printer in 2013 while he was studying at middle school. He used a robotic kit in his invention. There are other Braille printers on the market, but Banerjee's invention is just $350, and the other Braille printers cost around $2,000! He started his company, Braigo Labs, in 2014.

1 Look at the article. What is it about?

○ countries ○ inventions from the 20th century ○ people

2 7.03 Read and listen to the article. Then read the questions and write *AM* (Ann Makosinski) or *SB* (Shubham Banerjee).

Who ...

1 participated in events at school? SB
2 liked electronics as a child? ....
3 had the idea for an invention during a trip? ....
4 invented something at 12 years old? ....
5 was a winner at a science fair in 2013? ....
6 has a company? ....

3 Correct the sentences about the inventors in Exercise 1.

1 Ann Makosinski was born in the 21st century.
Ann Makosinski was born in the 20th century.
2 She invented a flashlight that uses batteries to create light.
....
3 She studied video games when she was a young teenager.
....
4 Shubham Banerjee participated in science fairs in middle school.
....
5 He used parts from an old printer in his invention.
....
6 His Braille printer costs $2,000.
....

THINK!

Think of Ann Makosinki's and Shubnam Banerjee's inventions. Which one do you prefer? Why?

WORKBOOK p.138

LANGUAGE IN CONTEXT

1 **Look at the examples below. Complete the sentences from the magazine article.**

Past Progressive and Simple Past	
when	Ann [1]........................ the Philippines **when** she **had** the idea for the flashlight.
while	Shubham [2]........................ the printer **while** he [3]........................ in middle school. She **was studying** electronics **while** her friends **were playing** video games.

2 **Complete the sentences. Use the past progressive form of the verbs.**

1 Dr. Taylor ....was working.... (work) in a hospital while she ....was living.... (live) in Germany.

2 The Spencers .... (stay) in a hotel while the workers .... (build) their new house.

3 I .... (write) an article about solar energy while my sister .... (listen) to music.

4 Mariela and Juan .... (use) my tablet while I .... (do) homework.

5 You .... (read) a book about Ada Lovelace while I .... (watch) a movie.

LOOK!

Don't forget to include the past of *to be* in past progressive sentences.

Alexander Fleming **was studying** bacteria when he discovered penicillin.

3 **Read the text and circle the correct options.**

Accidental Inventions and Discoveries that Changed the World!

Playdough (1950s): People [1]*used* / *were using* it to clean walls when a teacher [2]*started* / *was starting* to use it to make models in class.

Guide dogs for blind people (1918): A doctor's dog disappeared in a hospital. When he [3]*found* / *was finding* it, the dog [4]*guided* / *was guiding* a blind patient around the hospital.

Chocolate chip cookies (1930): Ruth Wakefield [5]*made* / *was making* chocolate cookies when she [6]*added* / *was adding* the wrong type of chocolate.

4 **Check (✓) the correct answer.**

1 I was taking a photo …
a when my cell phone fell in the pool. ◯
b while my cell phone was falling in the pool. ◯

2 The students were playing with playdough …
a when the teacher talked. ◯
b while the teacher was talking. ◯

USE IT!

5 **Work in pairs. Ask and answer questions about what you were doing at these times.**

1 last Sunday afternoon?
2 last night at 10 p.m.?
3 while your English teacher was explaining the last activity?

What were you doing last Sunday afternoon?

I was building a model.

LISTENING AND VOCABULARY

1 🔊 7.04 **Label the images with the words below. Then listen, check, and repeat.**

• ~~battery~~ • headphones • keyboard • printer • screen • tablet

1 

battery

2 

3 

4 

5 

6 

2 **Work in pairs. Look at objects 1–3 and tell your partner what you know about them.**

Guess the technology!

1 

2 

3 

3 🔊 7.05 **Listen to a game show about technology from the past. Which two objects from Exercise 2 did Sarah and Mark guess?**

○ DVD player ○ typewriter ○ Walkman®

4 🔊 7.05 **Listen again. Circle the correct options.**

1 Sarah is *excited* / *worried* about the game show.
2 Sarah and Mark can *listen to* / *look at* the products and they can touch them.
3 Sarah can see the product has a *keyboard* / *printer*, but it doesn't have *headphones* / *a screen* or batteries.
4 Sarah's *grandpa* / *mom* had a similar product, but his was electric.
5 Mark mentions the product's *batteries* / *headphones*.
6 Mark's answer is *correct* / *incorrect*.

WORKBOOK p.136 and 137

LANGUAGE IN CONTEXT

1 **Complete the question and the possessive pronouns from the game show in the chart. Use the words below.**

• hers • his • mine • ours • whose

Possessive Pronouns	
[1]............ turn is it?	It's [2]............ . It's **yours**. It's **his**. / It's **hers**. It's **ours**. It's **theirs**.
Singular	**Plural**
A **Whose** printer is **this**? B It's my printer. It's **mine**.	A **Whose** headphones are **these**? B They're my brother's. They're **his**.
My grandpa had a typewriter, but [3]............ was different. We have a printer, but [4]............ isn't similar to this.	They are similar to my sister's, only [5]............ are blue. They're our books. They're **ours**.

2 **Complete the mini dialogues with *whose* and the correct possessive pronouns. Look at the underlined words.**

1 A ....Whose.... pen is that?
B That's my pen. It's ....mine.....

2 A .... flashlight is this?
B It's Pedro's flashlight. It's ....

3 A .... car is this?
B It's my parents' car. It's ....

4 A .... book is that?
B That's your book. It's ....

3 **Circle the correct options.**

1 That isn't *my* / *mine* bike. I think it's Jenna's.
2 Hey, that is my tablet. *Your* / *Yours* is on the table!
3 This is my sister's notebook. *Her* / *Hers* name is on the cover.
4 *Our* / *Ours* classmates became famous!
5 They know our phone numbers, but we don't know *their* / *theirs*.
6 Excuse me, that's not your cell phone. It's *my* / *mine*.

USE IT!

4 **Choose three objects that three different classmates have. Write a description of each item in your notebook.**

• backpack • pencil case • sneakers

5 **Work in pairs. Take turns describing the objects in Exercise 4 and guessing whose they are.**

It's red and it's small.

Is it Luiza's pencil case?

No, it isn't. Hers is orange.

WORKBOOK p.136 and 138 PRACTICE EXTRA

AROUND THE WORLD

www.tourismestonia.com/tallinn/technology

Why Estonia | What to do | **Where to go** | What's special

Tallinn, the capital > *Technology*

Old Town in Tallinn

Why is Estonia Called E-stonia Now?

By Marina Campos

Estonia is a small country in the north of Europe. It has around 1.3 million people. Its capital, Tallinn, is a popular tourist destination, with a historic center – Old Town – that receives millions of visitors every year.

The country also attracts people and companies that work with technology and innovation. Estonia is becoming the most digital country in the world!

Let's look at some facts about the "Silicon Valley" of the Baltic Sea.

In 1997, the government created a plan to increase internet access in Estonia. In 1999, all the schools in the country had an internet connection.

Children start to learn how to program a computer when they are seven years old.

Estonians created Skype in 2003. Microsoft bought it for 8.5 billion dollars in 2011.

It's easy to find free wi-fi and people can go online even in rural areas.

Companies can test autonomous cars and robots in Estonia.

Public transportation is free in Tallinn for city residents. And there's free wi-fi on the buses, trams, trains, and ferries of course.

1 **Look at the article about Estonia. What is it about?**

◯ the geographic location of Estonia
◯ tourist attractions in Tallinn
◯ technology and innovation in Estonia

2 7.06 **Read and listen to the article. Write *T* (true) or *F* (false).**

In Estonia …

1 there is a large population. F
2 there is a city with old buildings. ....
3 internet expansion started in the 21st century. ....
4 teachers start to teach computer programming in middle school. ....
5 you can only access the Internet in big cities. ....
6 you can see an autonomous car on the street. ....

3 **Read the article again. Match numbers a–f with facts 1–6.**

a 1990s 3
b 1997 ....
c 7 ....
d 2003 ....
e 8.5 ....
f 1.3 ....

1 age students start to learn computer programming
2 amount of dollars (in billions) that Microsoft paid for Skype
3 decade of digital expansion in Estonia
4 number of people (in millions) that live in Estonia
5 the year of the plan to expand internet access
6 the year Skype started to operate

WORDS IN CONTEXT

4 **Complete the sentences with the words below.**

• go online • program • receive • test

1 Can you .... a microwave to cook food when you're not at home?
2 E-commerce companies want to .... delivery drones.
3 São Paulo and Rio de Janeiro .... millions of visitors every year.
4 I can't use my cell phone to .... in class.

THINK!

Compare the use of technology in your country to Estonia's. What are the similarities? What are the differences?

WEBQUEST

Learn more! What is Silicon Valley? Check (✓) *True* or *False*.

Silicon Valley is a region in California, USA, famous for its electronics and computer companies.

◯ **True** ◯ **False**

VIDEO

7.2

1 What was the first "computer" called?
2 What did Blaise Pascale do?

SPEAKING

TELLING AN ANECDOTE

1 7.07 **Read and listen to Isabela and Sousuke talking about a problem with a cell phone. Which image shows Isabela's problem?**

Sousuke	Hi, Isabela! Are you OK?
Isabela	No, I'm not. Something bad happened to me yesterday.
Sousuke	Oh no! What happened?
Isabela	My **cell phone fell in the swimming pool**.
Sousuke	You're kidding! How did that happen?
Isabela	Well, **it fell from my hand while I was texting**. I got really **angry**. My **cell phone** was **new**!
Sousuke	I'm sorry to hear that.

A

B

LIVING ENGLISH

2 **Complete the mini dialogues with the expressions below.**

- I'm sorry to hear that. • Well, • You're kidding!

1 A My sister didn't win a prize at the science fair.
  B .... She's so good at science.

2 A What happened to your tablet?
  B .... while I was riding my bike it fell from my bag.

3 A While I was doing the dishes, my new headphones fell in the sink.
  B ....

3 7.08 **Listen, check, and repeat the expressions.**

PRONUNCIATION

4 7.09 **Listen to how the final consonant sound of a word connects to the initial vowel sound of the next word in sentences.**

1 My cell phone fell in the swimming pool.
2 It fell from my hand while I was texting.

5 7.09 **Listen again and repeat the sentences.**

6 7.07 **Listen to the dialogue again. Then practice with a partner.**

7 **Role play a new dialogue. Follow the steps.**

1 Change the words in **blue** in Exercise 1 to write a new dialogue in your notebooks.
2 Practice your dialogue with a partner.
3 Present your dialogue to the class.

YOUR DIGITAL PORTFOLIO

Record your dialogue, then upload it to your class digital portfolio.

8 OUR NATURAL WORLD

UNIT GOALS

- Talk about the natural world and the weather.
- Read about changes in the environment.
- Listen to a weather report.
- Learn about deforestation.
- Write a poster for a clean-up event.

THINK!

1 Look at the photo. What is he/she doing?
2 What small things can we do to help nature?

VIDEO 8.1

1 Which four countries are in the video?
2 What is special about Guanabara Bay?

VOCABULARY IN CONTEXT

NATURE

1 8.01 **Read the pamphlets and label the images (1–10) with the words in bold. Then listen, check, and repeat.**

1 
grass

2 

3 

4 

5 

6 

7 

8 

9 

10 

2 **Think about your country, town, and neighborhood. Write the words in the chart.**

• birds • coast • fields • flowers • grass • hill • lake • trees • ocean • village

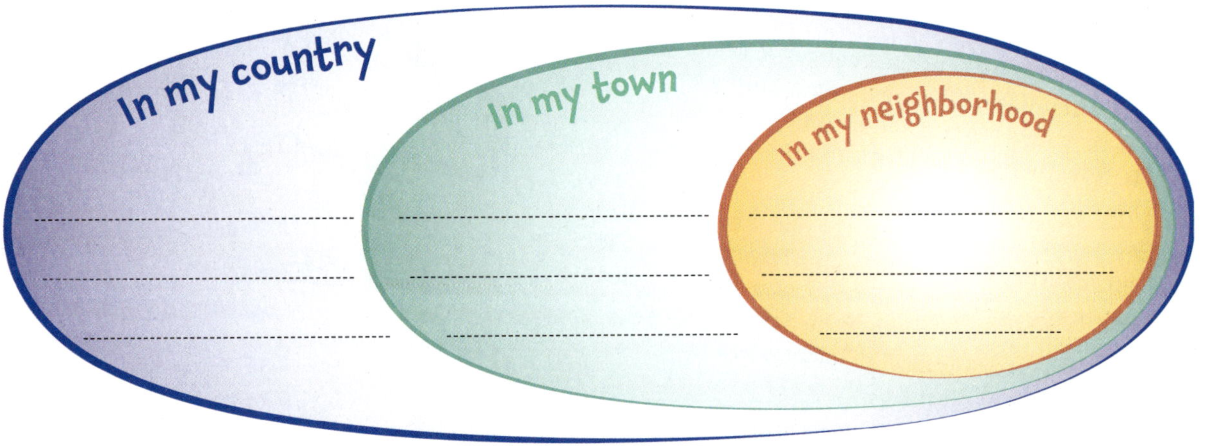

3 **Complete mind maps 1–4. Use the words/phrases below. You can use some words more than once.**

• along the coast • birds • flowers • hills • in the fields
• ~~in the lake~~ • in the ocean • in the village • on the grass • trees

USE IT!

4 **Make questions. Use the ideas in Exercise 3 with the correct form of the verbs.**

1 Do you like to ....?
2 Do you .... when you are on vacation?
3 Did you .... last weekend?
4 Were you .... at 6 p.m. yesterday?
5 How often do you..?

5 **Work in pairs. Ask and answer your questions in Exercise 4.**

Do you like to swim in the lake?

No, I don't. But I like to swim in the ocean.

WORKBOOK p.141 PRACTICE EXTRA

READING

Dear President,

I'm writing to tell you about the changes my family and I can see in our village. When my grandparents were teenagers, they loved to run and listen to the birds in the fields. Now there are no birds, and there is trash everywhere.

When my parents were children, the lake near our village was clean, and they could swim in it. They could see a lot of fish in the water, and they liked to play a game called "Count the Fish." They remember the day when they counted to a hundred! Today I'm lucky when I see one fish, but I see a lot of plastic in the water.

My friends and I wanted to do something about this. We talked to our teachers, and now we recycle a lot of things we use at school. Our teachers say our school wants to stop using plastic, but we need some funding to do that.

And I want to do more. I want to organize a group to clean up the lake. Can you give us some money for the bags and gloves we need to buy? The bags need to be recyclable, of course.

Thank you.

Ben Miller

1 Read the text quickly. Then complete the information about the text with the words below.

- a problem
- Ben
- ideas
- help
- ~~the president~~

The text is a letter to [1] *the president* . The author of the text is [2] .... The objectives of the text are to describe [3] .... , give some [4] .... , and ask for [5] ....

2 8.02 Read and listen to the text. Circle the correct options.

1 In the past, there were (*birds*) / *sheep* in the fields.
2 Ben's grandparents think the fields are *the same* / *different* now.
3 Ben's parents liked to play *in the ocean* / *in the lake* when they were children.
4 There are *a lot of* / *not many* fish near Ben's village now.
5 Ben and his friends *recycle* / *don't recycle* materials at their school.
6 Ben *has* / *doesn't have* bags and gloves to clean up the lake.

3 Complete the chart. Use the words below.

- ~~birds in the fields~~
- fish in the lake
- lake clean-up
- plastic in the water
- recycling at school
- trash in the fields

Past	Present	Future
birds in the fields		

THINK!

Is it important to know what your hometown or village looked like in the past? Why / Why not?

WORKBOOK p.143

LANGUAGE IN CONTEXT

1 **Look at the examples below. Complete the sentences from the letter.**

Verbs to Express Likes, Wants, and Needs

Simple Present	Simple Past
I **want** [1] to organize a group. You **love to listen** to the birds. Our school **wants** [2] ______ using plastic. We **like to talk** about recycling. The bags **need** [3] ______ recyclable.	I **needed to buy** bags and gloves. You **hated to see** trash in the lake. My granddad **loved to run** in the fields. My friends and I **wanted** [4] ______ something about this. They **liked** [5] ______ a game called "Count the Fish".

2 **Write sentences about images 1–4. Use the phrases below.**

- ~~Martina / want / look at birds / lake~~
- My dad and I / hate / see trash / the fields
- Lucas / love / run on the beach / dog
- Victor / want / go outside

1 Martina wants to look at birds near the lake.

2 ______

3 ______

4 ______

LOOK!

Remember to use *to* + the infinitive after verbs to express likes, wants, and needs.

I like **to** walk in the hills.

3 **Complete sentences 1–4 about four different places from the options below. Use *to* + the infinitive and your own ideas.**

1 I want ______ there.
2 I need ______ there.
3 I love ______ there.
4 I hate ______ there.

beach · coast · fields · hills · lake · ocean

USE IT!

I want to have a picnic there.

Do you want to go to the coast?

No, I don't.

4 **Work in pairs. Take turns to say your sentences from Exercise 3. Guess your partner's four places.**

LISTENING AND VOCABULARY

1 8.03 **Look at the images and complete labels 1–7 with the letters. Then listen and repeat.**

1 

r a i ny (i a)

2 

s .... ny (n u)

3 

cl .... dy (u o)

4 

st .... my (r o)

5 

f .... gy (o g)

6 

wi .... y (d n)

7 

s .... wy (n o)

2 8.04 **Listen to a weather report and check (✓) the correct details about the weather. Then compare your answers with a partner.**

Yesterday		Now		Later today		Tomorrow	
sunny	◯	cloudy	◯	cloudy with some rain	◯	windy and rainy	◯
rainy	✓	foggy	◯	stormy with some snow	◯	foggy and windy	◯
windy	◯	sunny	◯	windy with some fog	◯	hot and cloudy	◯

3 8.04 **Read comments 1–3 and then listen again. When did the person make each comment? Write *Y* (yesterday), *TD* (today), or *TM* (tomorrow).**

1 "I'm tired of wearing heavy clothes. I hate boots and coats! I want to wear sandals and T-shirts!" ....

2 "I'm worried about the weather. There's so much water around! Is it safe to drive home?" ....

3 "I'm angry. We started with a very nice day and I decided to have a picnic. But then the rain arrived and now we have to go home!" ....

4 **Complete the sentences with the weather words in Exercise 1.**

1 I'm not riding my bike today. It's ....foggy.... and I can't see anything.

2 I go to the beach every day in the summer. It's always .... here!

3 Last week it was very ...., and people couldn't leave their houses.

4 It's .... today and there's water everywhere, so I'm wearing my new boots.

5 We can't see the sun. It's really .... ! It's a gray day!

6 It's really .... ! Can you see the trees moving?

7 I love .... weather. I can play in the snow with my friends.

WORKBOOK p.140 and 141

LANGUAGE IN CONTEXT

1 Complete the sentences from the weather report in the chart. Use the words below.

• after • ~~and~~ • before • but • however • so

Connectors	
Addition	There's some cloudy weather moving in [1] ......and...... there's light rain in the afternoon.
Opposition	A I want to go for a walk by the river later! B Oh, [2] .... don't get too excited! We have the perfect weather for a walk! [3] ...., that changes in the afternoon …
Consequence	There's a possibility of snow showers, [4] .... don't forget to get your winter coats.
Time	Don't forget to get your winter coats [5] .... you go out tomorrow evening! [6] .... all that rainy weather yesterday I know everyone is a little worried.

2 Circle the correct options.

1 I was worried about the weather yesterday, *but / so* in the end it was OK: I got home before the snow.
2 The weather was horrible last weekend, *however, / so* I stayed home and played board games.
3 I check the weather on my cell phone *so / before* I leave for school every morning.
4 We are getting some rain this week *after / before* months and months with no rain.
5 It's a little cloudy now. *So / However,* the app says it's sunny!

3 Complete the conversation with connectors.

Hi! I arrived in Berlin today! It's awful here! It's snowy [1] .... windy!

Yeah … I'm staying at the hotel this evening, [2] .... the weather looks good tomorrow [3] .... I can explore the city then.

Great! But don't forget to check the weather [4] .... you leave the hotel!

USE IT!

4 Choose one of the options and complete the sentences so they are true for you. Then tell your partner.

1 I (*hate / don't hate*) rainy days, but ....
2 I (*want / don't want*) to spend my vacation in the country, so ....
3 I (*need / don't need*) to wear boots to walk in the hills. However, ...
4 I (*love / don't love*) to walk along the coast on windy days and ....

WORKBOOK p.140 and 142 PRACTICE EXTRA

ACROSS THE CURRICULUM

GEOGRAPHY

www.forumforindigenousteens.com

Home >> Forums >> Environment >> **Deforestation in Mexico – Argh!**

WorriedTeen

Posted 2 days ago

I'm just thinking about forests, and about why people are cutting down trees to create fields. I learned in school that there is deforestation in Mexico because people want to make fields for meat production. I'm very angry about it! How do you feel about deforestation in your country?

LIKE REPLY

Sonia

Posted 1 day ago

I'm from the Amazon. Deforestation is a big problem here today. I'm angry, too. And I'm worried about the water in the atmosphere. When we cut down trees, we have less rain. The Amazon needs the rain!

LIKE REPLY

Noor

Posted 4 hours ago

When we cut down the trees, animals die. I'm from Borneo, and we lost over 100,000 Bornean orangutans between 1999 and 2015. We don't want to lose more. Orangutans are so interesting! However, they need the forests to live – where can they go without the forests?

LIKE REPLY

KatofromUganda

Posted 2 hours ago

I live in Uganda, and we are losing a lot of our forests. Look!

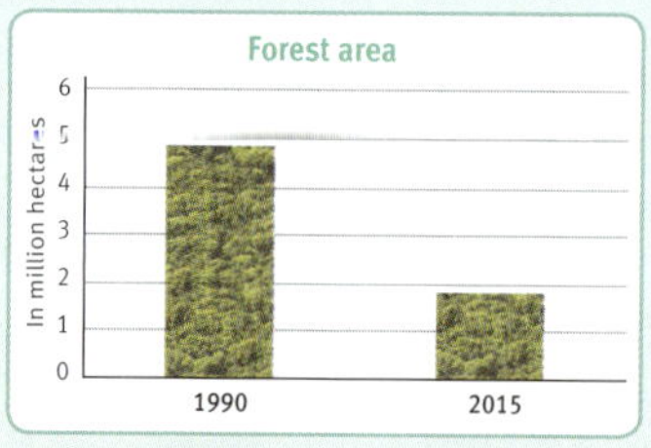

It's really bad: from 1990 to 2005 we lost about 63%! We need the forest for our food, and our home is here. And we use plants for medicines. My family and I need the forest to live, so I'm really worried.

LIKE REPLY

1 **Look at the online forum and check (✓) the correct answers.**

1 How many threads (or topics) are there in the text?
a one ◯ b three ◯ c four ◯

2 How many answers does the main post have?
a one ◯ b three ◯ c four ◯

3 Who wrote the main post?
a KatofromUganda ◯ b Noor ◯ c WorriedTeen ◯

4 What is the topic of the conversation?
a recycling ◯ b cutting down trees ◯ c the weather ◯

2 8.05 **Read and listen to the online forum. Then match the teenagers (1–3) with what they are worried about (a–c).**

1 Sonia ....
2 Noor ....
3 KatofromUganda ....

a the animals
b the people
c the water cycle

WORDS IN CONTEXT

3 **Match the words in bold (1–4) with their opposites (a–d).**

1 **cut down** trees ....
2 **less** rain ....
3 animals **die** ....
4 we don't want to **lose** more ....

a live
b more
c find
d plant

4 **Write *T* (true) or *F* (false) and justify your answers. Then compare with a partner.**

1 WorriedTeen writes about why people cut down trees in Mexico. ....T....
There is deforestation in Mexico because people want to make fields for meat production.

2 Sonia and Noor are from the same continent. ....
....

3 There is more water in the soil after deforestation. ....
....

4 Orangutans lose their homes when the forest is destroyed. ....
....

5 Some medicines are from plants. ....
....

5 **Answer the questions.**

1 Check (✓) the correct options.

a Opinions are …
◯ what a person thinks.
◯ what you can prove.

b Facts are …
◯ what a person thinks.
◯ what you can prove.

2 Circle the opinion and underline the fact in the sentences below.

Orangutans are so interesting! However, they need the forests to live.

3 Read the online forum again and underline two other facts.

WEBQUEST

Learn more! Check (✓) the correct answer.

We can find orangutans' natural habitats on …

◯ **only one continent.**
◯ **two continents.**
◯ **all the continents.**

THINK!

Write an answer to the post about deforestation in your country. Include your opinion and a fact in your answer.

VIDEO

8.2

1 How are animals' habitats similar to our homes?

2 Which two sea animals are in the video?

WRITING

CLEAN NEW CRESTON | Volunteer Group

DO YOU WANT TO MAKE A DIFFERENCE TO YOUR COMMUNITY?

WHAT CAN YOU DO? HERE ARE THREE IDEAS:

1. Join us on our clean-up events.
2. Donate! We need gloves and plastic bags, but remember: we only use recyclable plastic!
3. Post photos of this poster on social media.

NEXT CLEAN-UP EVENT
Central Park
November 29
9 a.m.–2 p.m.

Our last clean-up event in Gray Forest was a success!

- 26 volunteers collected 120 bags of trash.
- 52% of the trash collected went to recycling so we were all very happy!

EVERYONE NEEDS TO HELP KEEP OUR COMMUNITY CLEAN!

For more information visit www.cleannewcrestoncity.com or call John Ramirez at 0491667993.

1 Look at the poster. Check (✓) the correct answers.

1. Clean New Creston is a …
   a city. ◯ b school. ◯ c volunteer group. ◯
2. The authors of the poster are people from …
   a New Creston. ◯ b Gray Forest. ◯ c a recycling company. ◯
3. The objective of the poster is to …
   a give information about New Creston. ◯ b invite people to help New Creston. ◯

LOOK!

Ways of Talking to the Reader

The imperative:

Join us in our clean-up events.

2 8.06 Read and listen to the poster. What is the objective of each part of the poster? Match 1–6 with a–f.

1. The title b
2. A question ____
3. A large image ____
4. A list ____
5. A final line ____

a explains what people can do to help.
b shows who wrote the poster.
c invites people to read the rest of the poster.
d presents a problem.
e tells people how to learn more.

3 Study the Look! box. Underline one more example of a question with *you* and circle four more examples of the imperative in the poster.

4 Write a poster for a clean-up event.

1. Choose a problem to write about.
2. Collect information about the problem.
3. Write the first version of your poster.

5 Switch your poster with a partner, and check his/her work. Use the checklist below.

◯ title, a question, a list, an image, contact details
◯ verbs to express likes, wants, and needs
◯ connectors

YOUR DIGITAL PORTFOLIO

Edit your poster, then publish it. Upload it to the class portfolio for everyone to see!

REVIEW
UNITS 7 AND 8

VOCABULARY

1 **Write four verbs related to innovation. Use the letters below.**

~~b~~ c ~~d~~ d e f i i ~~l~~ l n n r s t ~~u~~ v v

1 b u i l d 2 _ _ _ _ o _ _ _ 3 _ _ y 4 _ _ _ e _ _

2 **Use the simple past form of the verbs in Exercise 1 to complete the sentences.**

Great Achievements Across History

- An airplane [1]............................ to the South Pole for the first time in 1956.
- Friedrich Miescher [2]............................ DNA in the 19th century.
- Mogul Emperor Shah Jahan [3]............................ the Taj Mahal from 1632 to 1643.
- Ralph Baer [4]............................ the video game in 1971.

3 **Look at the images and complete the sentences.**

1 

Look at the dog! He's sleeping on the ......grass......, under the ....

2 

There are beautiful red and yellow .... in the ....

3 

The .... are swimming in the ....

4 **Label the images to complete the weather chart.**

São Paulo, Brazil	 1	Chicago, United States	 3 ....
Sydney, Australia	 2	Mumbai, India	 4 ....

LANGUAGE IN CONTEXT

5 **Circle the correct options.**

What [1]*did you do* / *were you doing* when the teacher [2]*arrived* / *was arriving*?

I [3]*sent* / *was sending* a text message. But I put my phone in my backpack right away.

How [4]*did Mike fall off* / *was Mike falling off* his bike?

Well, he [5]*rode* / *was riding* his bike to school when he [6]*started* / *was starting* to feel sick.

6 **Look at the chart. Write questions and answers about objects 1–4 using *whose* and possessive pronouns.**

Objects	Owners	Objects	Owners
1 scooter	Pedro	3 T-shirts	Javier
2 video game	Haru and Akari	4 books	Becky

1 Mom Whose scooter is this? Is it Pedro's?

Becky Yes, it's his.

2 Mom ....

Becky ....

3 Mom ....

Becky ....

4 Mom ....

Becky ....

7 **Write the questions. Then answer them.**

1 you / want / go to the movies / this weekend / ?

Do you want to go to the movies this weekend?

....

2 what time / you / need / go to bed / on weekdays / ?

....

....

3 what / your best friend / like / do / on Sundays / ?

....

....

4 what food / you / hate / eat / ?

....

....

8 **Complete the sentences. Use the words below.**

- after
- before
- however
- so

1 Melissa goes to school in the mornings. .... she arrives home, she has lunch with her sister.

2 Do you always have breakfast .... you go to school?

3 Jackie needs to study for the math test tomorrow, ... she is in her bedroom right now.

4 The students usually go to the patio after lunch. .... , some of them prefer to read in the library.

CHECK YOUR PROGRESS

I CAN...

- talk about famous firsts and technology
- use the past progressive and simple past with *when/while*, and possessive pronouns
- talk about the natural world and the weather
- use verbs to express likes, wants, and needs, and use connectors.

LEARN TO LEARN

Record your vocabulary

Record yourself saying words you learned. Then record yourself saying them in sentences. Listen to your words and sentences every time you want to review vocabulary.

GLOBAL CHANGER EXTRAS

READING 1

ACROSS THE CURRICULUM / ART

STREET ART

1 Look at the title and the images. Answer the questions.

1 Where is this street art? ____________

2 What can you see in the images? ____________

Melbourne

STREET ART CAPITAL

Melbourne, in Australia, is famous for its colorful street art on many buildings downtown. You can visit Croft Alley in Chinatown – the Chinese neighborhood of Melbourne. Or go to Hosier Lane to see some amazing street art.

There are images of people next to animals and graffiti writing, but they don't stay the same. Street art often changes, and there are new images from one day to the next.

Street art in Hosier Lane

Are street art and graffiti different?

Yes, **graffiti** is usually words or letters. Graffiti artists use their tag (usually their name or a sign) to communicate with each other. **Street art** uses different techniques and materials, for example, stencils, sculpture, stickers, and posters. Some street artists only want to make beautiful murals, but other artists want to communicate what's happening in the world. Some street and graffiti artists work at night. The artist prepares a stencil or poster in a studio, and then uses it in the streets because it's fast.

Graffiti artists use tags

2 R.01 **Read and listen to the article. Check your answers to Exercise 1.**

3 Label images A–D with the street art techniques from the text.

A 

stickers

B 

____

C 

____

D 

____

4 Read the article again and answer the questions.

1 Where can you see street art in Melbourne?

In Croft Alley in Chinatown, and Hosier Lane

2 What is a tag?

____

3 What is the difference between street art and graffiti?

____

4 Why do street artists make street art?

____

5 Why do you think some street and graffiti artists work at night?

____

5 Find an image of graffiti or street art that you like. Describe it to a partner. Think about:

- the colors
- the shapes
- what it communicates
- why you like it.

THINK!

Talk about street art where you live. What type of street art or graffiti can you find? Do you like it?

READING 2

AROUND THE WORLD

CHINESE NEW YEAR

1 Look at the images. Discuss the questions with a partner.

1 What is Chinese New Year? 2 What things do people do at Chinese New Year?

2 R.02 Read and listen to the blog. Were your ideas in Exercise 1 correct?

ABOUT ME FASHION FOOD **FUN** STUDY TIPS

My favorite festival

By Lian

Chinese New Year lanterns

My favorite festival is Spring Festival. Some people also call it Chinese New Year. It's a big family **celebration** here in China. The date of the festival depends on the cycles of the moon. Some years it is in January and others in February.

Before the festival, we clean and **decorate** our houses. Every neighborhood, street, and building has red decorations. We love the color red as it is a symbol of energy and being happy.

The Spring Festival dinner is very important. Many Chinese people travel to be with their families. We eat special food together. Parents and grandparents often give children red **envelopes** with money. You take the envelope with both hands. It isn't **polite** to use one hand or to open the envelope in front of the person. Today, a lot of people also send red envelopes to friends and family online.

Many cities and towns in China celebrate Spring Festival with **fireworks**, dragon and lion dances, and fairs at parks. My favorite thing about Spring Festival is seeing the bright colors of the fireworks at night. They're beautiful!

Red envelopes with money

3 Read the blog again and answer the questions.

1 Why does the date of Chinese New Year change every year?
   Because the date depends on the cycles of the moon.
2 Why do Chinese people use red decorations?
   ....
3 What do children get from their families for New Year?
   ....
4 How do children take their presents?
   ....
5 How can people get presents in another country?
   ....

4 Complete the sentences. Use the words in bold in the blog.

1 We put special lanterns in our house to *decorate* it for Spring Festival.
2 Do you have some ....? I need to send some letters.
3 I love watching the colors of the .... and listening to the loud sounds!
4 We had a big .... for my 18th birthday.
5 In my country, it isn't .... to eat with your mouth open.

THINK!

Is Chinese New Year similar to a festival in your country? What's different?

READING 3

ACROSS THE CURRICULUM / MATH

OUR GREAT TRAIN ADVENTURE!

1 **Look at the title and the chart. Answer the questions.**

1 Which three countries did this train go through?

2 Which four main towns did the train go through?

2 R.03 **Read and listen to the travel journal. Check your answers to Exercise 1.**

The Trans-Mongolian Express

We decided to take the Trans-Mongolian Express train to see the small towns and villages of Siberia. We were very excited!

→ **Tuesday, March 21** *Our trip started in Moscow. It was Tuesday night when we got on the train. There were many people at the station. At 23:45, the train left Moscow.*

→ **Wednesday, March 22** *The train stopped at different stations. It was night again when we stopped at Perm. It's famous for its ballet and literature.*

→ **Thursday, March 23 and Friday, March 24**
After 25 hours, we arrived at Yekaterinburg, on the border between Europe and Asia. Then we traveled across Siberia.

→ **Saturday, March 25 and Sunday, March 26**
We stopped at Irkutsk and saw the amazing Lake Baikal. We crossed the Russian-Mongolian border and arrived at Ulaanbaatar, the capital of Mongolia. When we traveled through the Gobi desert, we saw people on horseback.

There were often people selling food and drink at the stations, but we ate on the train. There was a Russian restaurant while the train was in Russia and a Mongolian restaurant in Mongolia. Then it changed to a Chinese restaurant in China. We tried lots of different foods!

→ **Monday, March 27** *The train crossed the mountains and we saw the Great Wall of China. Six nights and seven days later, we arrived in Beijing. It was a fantastic experience!*

RUSSIA	MOSCOW	0 KM
	PERM	1,378 KM
	YEKATERINBURG	1,777 KM
	IRKUTSK	5,152 KM
MONGOLIA	ULAANBAATAR	6,265 KM
CHINA	BEIJING	7,621 KM

3 **Read the travel journal again and answer the questions.**

1 Where did the trip start? In Moscow.

2 What did they see near Irkutsk?

3 What did they see in the Gobi desert?

4 Where did the writer eat?

4 **Answer the questions.**

1 Which day of the week did they leave Moscow? Tuesday

2 What was the distance between Yekaterinburg and Irkutsk?

3 How far did they travel from Ulaanbaatar to Beijing?

4 How many days did it take to arrive in Ulaanbaatar?

5 How far did they travel from Moscow to Beijing?

THINK!

Why do some people prefer to travel long distances by train? Do you? Where can you travel to by train in your country?

READING 4

AROUND THE WORLD

LIFE ON A FARM IN CANADA

1 Look at the images. Discuss the questions with a partner.

1 Who are these people?

2 What is their life like?

2 R.04 Read and listen to the blog. Were your ideas in Exercise 1 correct?

ABOUT ME OUR FARM FAMILY LIFE FOOD FUN

My name's Felix Nagy. This is my blog about life on our eco-farm.

My mom, dad, sister, and I live on a farm in Canada. Before we **moved** to the farm, we lived in the city of Quebec. It was very different. My mom and dad both had jobs and they were always **busy**, so they weren't at home very much.

One summer, they decided to buy a farm. We went to live in a beautiful place in the country, outside Quebec.

My mom and dad built parts of the house. We have solar panels for electricity and big tanks for the **rainwater**. They also created a big garden.

My sister and I started at the high school. It's really **far**, so we go by bus every day. At first it was difficult because we didn't know anyone, but now there are always teenagers at our house!

When we're not at school, we help on the farm. We get all of our food from the garden. We have chickens for eggs and lots of fruit and vegetables.

I don't have a cell phone, and we all share one computer. But it's never boring. One day, I was taking photos of the garden when I saw a huge snake in the grass. **Luckily**, it wasn't dangerous!

3 Read the blog again and answer the questions.

1 Where did the family live at first?

In the city of Quebec.

2 Why did Felix's parents want to change their life?

....

3 What is special about the house the family live in?

....

4 How do the children go to school?

....

5 Where do they get their food from?

....

6 What do the children do when there isn't school?

....

4 Complete the sentences. Use the words in bold in the blog.

1 You can use ...rainwater... to water the plants.

2 My house isn't very .... from the grocery store.

3 They had a car accident, but .... they were all OK.

4 Our grandparents .... from their house to an apartment.

5 I'm sorry, I don't have time. I'm too ....

THINK!

Talk about the differences between life in a city and on a farm. Is Felix's life different from yours? What's different?

PUZZLES & GAMES

UNIT 1

1 **Find seven places in town (→, ↓, ↗, ↘).**

D	V	S	K	A	T	E	P	A	R	K	G	K
M	U	I	W	A	Q	E	H	Z	X	B	R	X
V	O	U	T	O	W	X	W	X	Y	O	O	R
X	T	V	S	P	O	T	L	J	I	W	C	R
G	I	D	I	T	O	L	V	M	X	L	E	U
F	U	G	G	E	A	Q	B	X	J	I	R	L
D	S	O	A	M	T	D	S	R	M	N	Y	M
N	F	S	P	B	W	H	I	X	S	G	S	I
F	H	H	P	R	P	W	E	U	G	A	T	N
V	I	V	R	U	A	D	P	A	M	L	O	O
A	U	V	B	O	R	H	R	F	T	L	R	W
S	H	O	Z	B	K	I	W	X	O	E	E	X
V	I	F	T	C	T	M	V	G	Y	Y	R	H

2 **Read sentences a–f. Then use the words in bold to label buildings 1–7.**

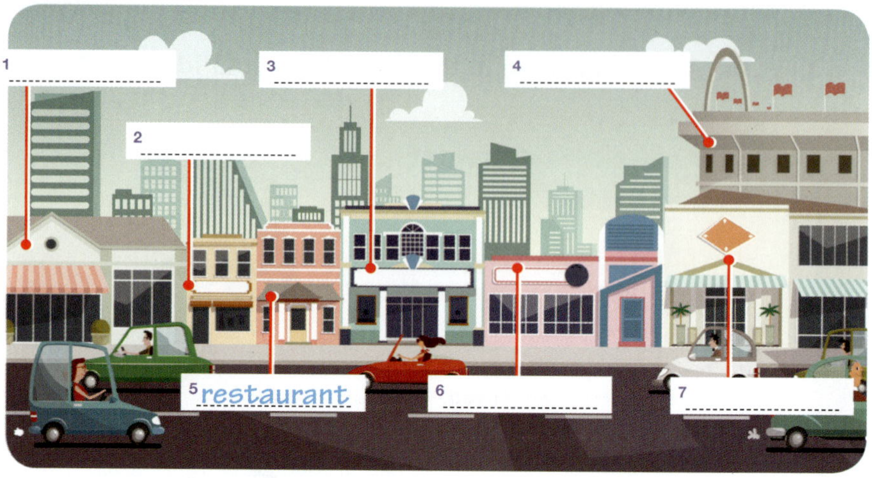

a There's a **movie theater** next to Li's Chinese **restaurant**.

b The bowling alley is between the **mall** and the **movie theater**.

c The **clothing store** is next to Li's Chinese **restaurant**.

d The **mall** is in front of the **stadium**.

e There is no building on the right of the **stadium**.

f The **clothing store** is between a **restaurant** and the **grocery store**.

UNIT 2

3 **Look at the images and complete the crossword. What's the secret food word?**

1 

2 

3 

4 

5 

6 

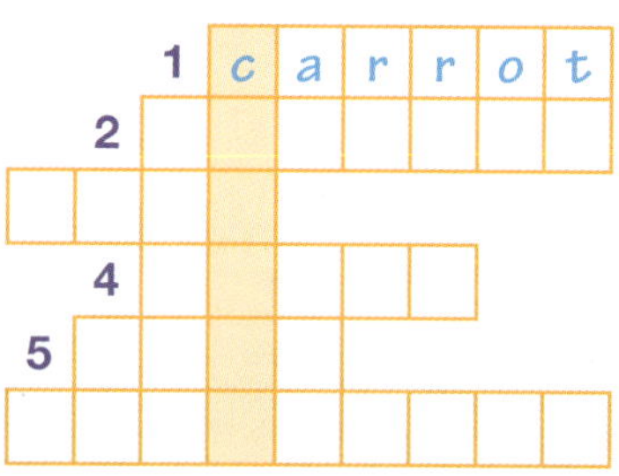

The secret food word is ....

4 **Look at sentences a and b and complete the code in the chart. Then write sentences a–g using the code and answer the question.**

1	2	3	4	5	6	7	8	9	10	11	12	13	14	15	16	17	18	19
d	......	c	g	i	......	u	......	s	o	k	f	m	r	x	......	l	n	y

a 4 2 8   6   12 10 14 11

....   a   ....

b 13 5 15   8 16 2   2 4 4 9

....   t h e   ....

c 6 1 1   9 6 17 8

....

d 3 7 8   6 18 10 18 5 10 18

....

e 12 14 19   8 16 2   10 18 5 10 18

....

f 6 1 1   8 16 2   2 4 4 9

....

g 12 14 19   8 16 2   2 4 4 9
6 18 1   10 18 5 10 18

....
....

What are the instructions for?

....

UNIT 3

1 **Use the code to write the words.**

1 b e a c h

2 ______ ______

3 ______

4 ______ ______

5 ______

2 **Use the words with the same color. Put the words in order and add *a*, *at*, *on*, *the* to make questions. Then answer the questions about the Amazing Safari Hotel.**

there	swimming pool	night safari?	there	restaurants
tour guides	there	Were	hotel?	Was
Were	two	fishing	and	two
kayaking	Was	hotel?	there	river?

1 Was there a swimming pool at the hotel?

2 ______

3 ______

4 ______

UNIT 4

3 **Cross out the words for each question a–h in the diagram and write the words. Then answer questions.**

a 2 types of fruit orange ______

b 3 buildings

______ ______ ______

c 3 things you wear

______ ______ ______

d 3 types of food

______ ______ ______

e 2 things you do with your mouth open

______ ______

1 Which word isn't crossed out? ______

2 Write a sentence using this word.

______

4 **Complete the text with the simple past of the irregular verbs. Then write the answer.**

Daniel [1] read (read) this puzzle yesterday, but he couldn't find the answer. Can you help him?

A man and his son [2] ______ (be) in their car when they [3] ______ (have) an accident. An ambulance [4] ______ (take) the boy to the hospital. They [5] ______ (go) very fast. But when the ambulance arrived, the doctor [6] ______ (see) the young boy and [7] ______ (say), "I can't operate. He's my son." How is that possible?

Answer:

______

UNIT 5

1 **Use the code to find the first and last letters of the means of transportation. Then write the words 1–9.**

	1	2	3	4	5
A	A	B	C	D	E
B	F	G	H	I	J
C	K	L	M	N	O
D	P	Q	R	S	T
E	U	V	W	X	Y

1 A1 A5 a e airplane
2 B1 E5 ....
3 D4 D3 ....
4 A2 D5 ....
5 D4 E5 ....
6 C3 A5 ....

2 **Put the words in the same color in order to make questions 1–4. Then answer the questions for you.**

it, Did, night?, walk, you, last, rain, TV, go, week?, pool, you, last, on, swimming, Did, watch, Did, last, Monday?, to, to, Did, weekend?, you, school, a

1 Did you go to a swimming pool last weekend?
Yes, I did.

2 ....

3 ....

4 ....

UNIT 6

3 **Complete the crossword with the correct personality adjective to describe each person. What's the secret word?**

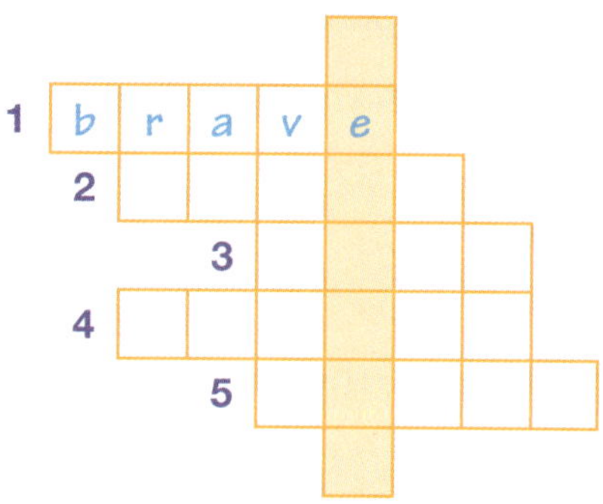

1 This person isn't scared.
2 This person is intelligent.
3 This person does good things for other people.
4 This person has big muscles.
5 This person makes you laugh

The secret word is ....

4 **Look at the photos from 11 a.m. last Sunday. What were these people doing? Read sentences 1–6 and write the names.**

11 a.m. last Sunday

1 Sergio wasn't helping his sister.
2 Maria was in the kitchen, but she wasn't cooking.
3 Victor wasn't cooking. His dad was listening to music.
4 Gabriela was helping her brother.
5 Isabela and her Mom were dancing.
6 Mario wasn't listening to music.

UNIT 7

1 Add vowels to the letters to make the infinitive of verbs related to innovation. Then complete the sentences with the correct simple past form.

In 1774, William Herschel [1] built (bld) a big telescope. He [2] .... (s) the telescope to look at stars and planets. In 1781, he [3] .... (dscvr) the planet Uranus and he [4] .... (bcm) famous. Later, he [5] .... (strt) making telescopes.

2 Read sentences a–f. Check (✓) the information in the chart and complete sentences 1–3.

a Raquel was working inside.

b Camila was outside when it started to rain.

c Helena wasn't outside the clothing store when it started to rain.

d This person was waiting for a bus outside the clothing store.

e This person was having lunch in a cafeteria in a store.

f This person was in the teachers' lounge.

	What they were doing			Place		
	Working	Waiting for a bus	Eating a sandwich	Outside the clothing store	In the mall	At the school
Name Raquel	✓					
Camila						
Helena						

1 It started to rain while Raquel ....

2 Camila ....

when ....

3 It .... while Helena ....

UNIT 8

3 Find ten words about nature.

V	B	I	R	D	S	F	Q	L	I
L	I	S	P	J	U	X	O	L	D
S	B	L	T	S	A	O	C	I	D
P	S	S	L	E	M	W	E	H	O
G	X	A	E	A	F	U	A	E	L
V	C	R	R	I	G	R	N	T	A
D	B	M	E	G	S	E	E	R	K
G	R	L	U	W	A	J	X	E	E
Y	D	T	Z	F	T	L	U	E	D
S	R	E	W	O	L	F	Z	S	Z

4 Dan and his friends like to do different activities on the weekend. Read sentences a–f and check (✓) the information in the chart. Then complete sentences 1–3 about last weekend.

	garden	lake	beach
Dan			
Noah			
Elena			

a *Elena loves to read outside.*

b *Dan didn't take his dog to the lake.*

c *Noah likes to swim.*

d *Dan loves to run with his dog near water.*

e *Elena likes to look at birds and flowers.*

f *Noah didn't go to the beach.*

1 *Dan* ....

2 *Elena* ....

3 *Noah* ....

PROJECT
THE STORY OF A PAINTING

MAKE AN AUDIO GUIDE FOR A FAMOUS PAINTING.

1 Look at the painting and the text of the audio guide quickly. Check (✓) the correct answers.

1 Where do you think you can listen to the audio guide?
- ◯ on a tourist bus
- ◯ in a museum

2 What is the audio guide for?
- ◯ to give information about the artist's life
- ◯ to give information about the artist's life and the painting

2 Work in pairs. Look at the painting and answer the questions.

1 What can you see in the painting?

....

2 How many people are there?

....

3 What is happening?

....

4 How does the painting make you feel?

....

5 Where do you think the painting is? Why?

....

3 P.01 **Read and listen to the audio guide. Answer the questions and complete the sentences.**

1 Monet was from ....France.... (Which country?)
2 Monet moved to the house in the painting in .... (Which year?)
3 Monet painted it in .... (Which village?)
4 The boy next to the toy in the painting is .... (Who?)
5 Monet often painted .... (What?)
6 Monet planted .... in the garden at Vétheuil. (What?)
7 Monet had .... children. (How many?)

THINK!

Do you like the painting? Why / Why not? What do you know is important to Monet?

PROJECT TASK

1 PLAN

1 Choose a famous painting.
2 Find out about the painting. Look for images.
3 Write your audio guide. Remember to include information about the painter, what you can see in the painting, and why the things/people in the painting were important to the painter.
4 Check grammar, spelling, punctuation, and practice your pronunciation of difficult words.
5 Record your audio guide.

2 YOUR DIGITAL PORTFOLIO

Upload your audio guide to the class portfolio for everyone to see and hear! Present your audio guide to the class.

3 REFLECT

Which is your favorite audio guide? Why?

Claude Monet (1840–1926),
The Artist's Garden at Vétheuil: 1881
Oil on canvas, 151.5 x 121 cm

The painting, *The Artist's Garden at Vétheuil*, 1881, is by the French Impressionist painter, Oscar-Claude Monet. He was born in 1840 and died in 1926. The house in the painting was in the small village of Vétheuil in France. In 1878, Monet went to live there with his wife, Camille, his son, Jean, and his son, Michel. Soon after they arrived in Vétheuil, Monet's wife died, but Monet stayed in Vétheuil with his two boys.

Monet painted a lot of his paintings outside, and he often painted his garden in different light and at different times of the day. Monet loved to plant flowers where he lived. In the garden in Vétheuil, he planted tall flowers, and the blue and white flowerpots in the painting were Monet's. He took them with him every time he changed house and they are in many of his paintings. Look closely at the flowerpots. What different colors can you see? The boy in the painting next to a toy is Monet's son, Michel. We don't know who the woman was in the painting. The painting has many bright colors, but it was a sad time in Monet's life.

PROJECT
DESCRIBING AN ANIMAL

MAKE A PAMPHLET ABOUT AN ANIMAL IN DANGER.

1 Look at the images and the text of the pamphlet quickly. Check (✓) the correct answers.

1 What is the objective of the pamphlet?
- ◯ to teach people about the problem with Scarlet Macaws
- ◯ to teach people about birds in South America

2 What type of information does it have?
- ◯ opinion ◯ factual

2 Read the pamphlet and complete the fact file.

Fact File	
Description	big, red, ...
Size	
Habitat	
Diet	
Babies	

3 Read the pamphlet again and answer the questions.

1 What problem does the pamphlet describe?

....

2 What is the reason for the problem?

....

3 What does the volunteer group do to help the Scarlet Macaws?

....

4 Do you think the pamphlet is attractive? Why?

....

PROJECT TASK

1 PLAN

1 Choose an animal in danger in your local area.
2 Find out about the animal. Look for images.
3 Write your text. Remember to include a description of the animal, its habitat and diet, the main problems, and possible solutions.
4 Design your pamphlet.
5 Check grammar, spelling, and punctuation.

THINK!

Why are many animals in danger? Do you do anything to protect animals in danger?

2 YOUR DIGITAL PORTFOLIO

Upload your pamphlet to the class portfolio for everyone to see! Present your pamphlet to the class.

3 REFLECT

Which is your favorite pamphlet? Why?

ALERT
Every year more Scarlet Macaws disappear. Help us save this beautiful bird. Join our volunteer group now!

HELP PROTECT SCARLET MACAWS

The Scarlet Macaw (*Ara macao*) is a big, red, yellow, and blue parrot. A Scarlet Macaw can be 85–96 cms from head to tail and it can weigh about 1 kg.

Where it lives

It usually lives in the forests of tropical South America, in countries such as Mexico, Peru, Bolivia, and Brazil. Scarlet Macaws usually build their nests in holes in trees. They eat big seeds, fruit, and some leaves with their strong beaks. They sometimes eat insects.

Babies

Female Scarlet Macaws have one or two baby birds every two years. Both parents teach and take care of the baby birds. They are social animals and they live their whole life with the same partner. They often live in groups of three or four. They can live for 50 years in the wild.

The problem

Scarlet Macaws are losing their habitat because of deforestation. It is illegal, but some people also catch and sell these beautiful animals as pets.

What can we do?

We plant new forests where Scarlet Macaws can live.
We organize groups in local communities to take care of the Scarlet Macaws.
To join our volunteer group contact José Luís: info@savethemacaws.org

IRREGULAR VERBS

Infinitive	Simple Past
be	was / were
beat	beat
become	became
begin	began
break	broke
bring	brought
build	built
buy	bought
catch	caught
choose	chose
come	came
cost	cost
cut	cut
do	did
draw	drew
drink	drank
drive	drove
eat	ate
fall	fell
feel	felt
fight	fought
find	found
fly	flew

Infinitive	Simple Past
forget	forgot
get	got
give	gave
go	went
grow	grew
have	had
hear	heard
hide	hid
hit	hit
hold	held
keep	kept
know	knew
leave	left
lose	lost
make	made
meet	met
pay	paid
put	put
read	read
ride	rode
ring	rang
run	ran
say	said

Infinitive	Simple Past
see	saw
sell	sold
send	sent
shut	shut
sing	sang
sit	sat
sleep	slept
speak	spoke
spend	spent
stand	stood
swim	swam
take	took
teach	taught
tell	told
think	thought
throw	threw
understand	understood
wake	woke
wear	wore
win	won
write	wrote

WORKBOOK CONTENTS

1 AROUND TOWN

LANGUAGE REFERENCE

There is/There are: Affirmative, Negative, *Yes/No* Questions, and Short Answers

Affirmative (+)	Negative (–)
There is a bowling alley in my town.	**There isn't** a stadium in my town.
There are three parks in my town.	**There aren't** skateparks in my town.

Yes/No Questions (?)	Short Answers	
Is there a mall in your town?	Yes, **there is**.	No, **there's not**. / No, **there isn't**.
Are there movie theaters in your town?	Yes, **there are**.	No, **there aren't**.

We use *isn't* or *aren't* in the negative form. We use *'s not / isn't* or *aren't* in the short answers negative form.

Adverbs of Frequency

		How often do you go to the grocery store?
100%	I **always** go to the skatepark on Saturday.	I go **every** day.
	Carolina **often** wears sneakers.	I go **every** weekend.
	We **sometimes** play volleyball on the weekend.	I go **once a** week.
0%	My brothers **never** go to the mall.	I go **twice a** week.
		I **never** go to the grocery store.

Places in Town

bowling alley
clothing store
grocery store
mall
movie theater
park
skatepark
stadium

Prepositions of Place

behind
between
in front of
inside
left
next to
right

VOCABULARY

1 Label images 1–6 with the words/phrases below.

• bowling alley • clothing store • grocery store • park • skatepark • ~~stadium~~

1

stadium

2

3

4

5

6

2 Put the letters in the correct order and write the places.

1 There is food in this store.
cregory otser grocery store

2 We watch movies here.
voime heettar ....

3 There are shops and restaurants here.
lalm ....

4 We walk and play soccer here.
rapk ....

5 We watch soccer games here.
satdumi ....

6 There are jackets, jeans, and shirts in this store.
tlochngi soter ....

3 Circle the correct options.

1

They are *in front of* / *inside* their house.

2

Ana is on the *left* / *right* and Gabriel is on the *left* / *right*.

3

Dad is *next to* / *between* Isaac and Felipe.

4

Maria is *next to* / *behind* Mom.

5

The cat is *inside* / *in front of* the box.

6

A man is *behind* / *in front of* the door.

GRAMMAR

1 Complete the sentences with *is*, *are*, *isn't*, or *aren't*.

1 There ......are...... two malls in my town.
2 There .... a movie theater next to the hotel.
3 A .... there some restaurants near here?
B No, there ....
4 There .... grocery stores in my town. We buy food in the city.
5 .... there parks in your town?
6 A .... there a skatepark in this town?
B No, there ....

2 Complete the dialogue with the phrases below.

• are there • is there • there are • ~~there is~~ • there is • there isn't

Camila Do you like your new neighborhood, Victor?

Victor Yes, I love it! It's modern and [1] ......there is...... a nice park.

Camila And [2] .... a skatepark in the park?

Victor No, [3] .... , but [4] .... a bowling alley next to the park.

Camila Cool! But [5] .... movie theaters?

Victor Yes, [6] .... two great movie theaters.

Camila That's awesome! I love to watch movies.

3 Match 1–5 with a–e.

1 We play soccer once ...e...
2 I go to the skatepark twice ......
3 Enzo is very healthy. He never ......
4 Amanda takes a shower every ......
5 Enzo is very healthy. He always ......

a drinks water.
b day.
c a week, on Tuesday and Thursday.
d eats junk food.
e a week, on Saturday.

4 Put the words in the correct order.

1 a week / Sofia / go to / and I / movie / the / theater once
......Sofia and I go to the movie theater once a week......
2 games every / My / plays / brother / video / day
....
3 restaurants / go / I sometimes / to / friends / with my
....
4 never / her / does / homework / dinner / Juliana / after
....
5 goes to / Carla / the / her mom / often / with / grocery store
....
6 on the / always / Alex / the / goes to / skatepark / weekend
....

READING

1 Look at the texts and check (✓) the correct answers.

1 What are they about?
- ◯ two homes
- ◯ a hotel and another similar place

2 What are they for?
- ◯ to give information
- ◯ to ask for information

Review ★★

This is a nice apartment – it's big and modern. There is only one problem: it's very boring near here! There aren't restaurants or cafés in the neighborhood. (We have breakfast and dinner in the apartment every day.) 😒 There is only one small grocery store. There's a park behind the apartment, but it's very small, too, and there isn't a skatepark. It's OK for one or two days, but I don't recommend it for a week.

Nozomi
From Tokyo, Japan.

Review ★★★★★

Our room in this old hotel is very small, but the neighborhood is awesome! There are a lot of restaurants (six on this street)! There is a really nice pizza restaurant next to the hotel. (We are eating a lot of pizza this evening!) 😊 There are three movie theaters. There's a beautiful big park, too. We hang out there every day. I really recommend it – I don't want to go home!

David
From Madrid, Spain.

2 Read the texts and write *T* (true) or *F* (false) next to the statements.

1 Nozomi likes the apartment's neighborhood. F
2 Nozomi likes the apartment. ....
3 There are a lot of grocery stores near the apartment. ....
4 The park is in front of the apartment. ....
5 David likes the hotel's neighborhood. ....
6 David always has dinner in the hotel. ....
7 David goes to the park every day. ....
8 The park near David's hotel is small. ....

3 Write answers to the questions.

1 Where does Nozomi have breakfast and dinner?
She has breakfast and dinner in the apartment.

2 How many places to buy food are there near Nozomi's apartment?
....

3 Where is the park near Nozomi's apartment?
....

4 What food does David like?
....

5 How many places to watch movies are there near David's hotel?
....

2 DELICIOUS DIVERSITY

LANGUAGE REFERENCE

Can for Permission: Affirmative, Negative, *Yes/No* Questions, and Short Answers

Affirmative (+)	Negative (–)
I **can wear** jeans to school. You **can use** your cell phone in class. He/She **can eat** and drink in class. We **can play** video games at school. They **can use** their teachers' first names.	I **can't wear** jeans to school. You **can't use** your cell phone in class. He/She **can't eat** and drink in class. We **can't play** video games at school. They **can't use** their teachers' first names.
***Yes/No* Questions**	**Short Answers**
Can I **wear** jeans to school? **Can** you **use** your cell phone in class? **Can** he/she **eat** and drink in class? **Can** we **play** video games at school? **Can** they **use** their teachers' first names?	Yes, I **can**. / No, I **can't**. Yes, you **can**. / No, you **can't**. Yes, he/she **can**. No, he/she **can't**. Yes, we **can**. / No, we **can't**. Yes, they **can**. / No, they **can't**.

We use *can* and *can't* to talk about permission.

Making Suggestions and Responding

Making Suggestions	Responding
How about making a pizza?	**Great/Good idea!** I love pizza.
Let's add some beans.	**Sure!** **Well**, I don't really like fried chicken.
Why don't I fry the chicken?	**Don't worry**, I can fry the chicken.

Subject and Object Pronouns

Subject Pronouns	Object Pronouns
I love cheese.	Please, tell **me** your name.
You go to bed at eight o'clock.	I'm helping **you**.
He eats fish.	I like **him**.
She plays soccer.	Please give **her** the fork.
It runs fast.	Put **it** here, please.
We like pizza.	Mrs. Silva teaches **us** English.
They have dinner at seven o'clock.	I can see **them**.

Food

beans
carrot
cheese
chicken
fish
orange juice
pineapple
rice

Cooking

add
cut
fork
fry
knife
mix
onion
salt

VOCABULARY

1 Find six words for food.

soligcarrottburtytirericedbeansporthelcheesemopreadchickentirebirfishedhop

1 carrot
2 ....
3 ....
4 ....
5 ....
6 ....

2 Match 1–8 with a–h.

1 beans e
2 carrot ....
3 cheese ....
4 chicken ....
5 fish ....
6 orange juice ....
7 pineapple ....
8 rice ....

a

b

c

d

e

f

g

h

3 Look at images 1–5. Complete the labels with the words below.

• add • cut • fork • ~~fry~~ • mix • onion • salt

1

fry the ....

2

.... the eggs

3

.... the chicken

4

.... the ....

5

knife and ....

GRAMMAR

1 **Complete the sentences with *can* or *can't* and the verbs below.**

• do • ~~eat~~ • go • listen • use • wear

1 We ....can't eat.... junk food at home. (–)
2 I .... to bed after ten o'clock on the weekend. (+)
3 You .... your cell phone at school. (–)
4 .... we .... sneakers to school? (?)
5 .... they .... their homework at school? (?)
6 We .... to music in the school cafeteria. (+)

2 **Match 1–5 with a–e.**

1 Let's ...c...
2 How about ....
3 Why don't I ....
4 Yes. Great ....
5 Don't worry, ...

a cooking some fish?
b idea!
c add some cheese.
d I can do that.
e mix the eggs?

3 **Complete the sentences with the correct subject pronoun. Then match them with images A–E.**

1 I don't want this pizza, Theo. ....You.... can have it.
2 Abigail and I are having breakfast. .... are in the kitchen.
3 Logan and Oliver are in the library. .... are doing their homework.
4 My sister is in her bedroom. .... is getting up.
5 My dad is cooking. .... is frying some fish.

A

B

C

D

E

4 **Circle the correct word.**

1 Beatriz plays soccer. She loves (*it*) / *him*.
2 I don't understand this exercise. Can you help *I* / *me*, please?
3 Who is that man? Do you know *him* / *he*?
4 Mrs. Cheng is a very nice teacher. I like *she* / *her*.
5 Mason and Nicolas are here. I can see *them* / *they*.

READING

1 Look at the text and check (✓) the correct answers.

1 What is it?
- ◯ a blog post
- ◯ an article

2 What is it about?
- ◯ dinnertime in two families
- ◯ the food that families eat

WHAT'S FOR DINNER?

Today two young readers, Gabriela (12) and Laura (13), tell us about dinnertime in their houses.

GABRIELA From Monday to Friday, I have dinner with my family (my mom, dad, and my two sisters, Ana and Juliana). We eat at the big table in our kitchen. We often talk about music, sports, clothes – a lot of different things. We don't always talk about school! We can't look at a cell phone or a book during dinner. Mom says it's our time to talk as a family. It's different on the weekend – we can have dinner in the living room. On Saturday, we sometimes watch TV and eat dinner at the same time.

LAURA I have dinner with my dad and brother every day of the week. We eat in our dining room. I talk with my dad – I tell him about my day at school. My brother often reads a book during dinner. He loves books. My dad says we can't use a cell phone during dinner, but we can read.

2 Read the text and write *G* (Gabriela) or *L* (Laura).

1 This person eats in the kitchen. G
2 This person eats in the dining room. ....
3 This person often talks about her day at school. ....
4 This person often talks about music. ....
5 Who can't read at dinner? ....
6 Who can eat in the living room on the weekend? ....

3 Write answers to the questions.

1 Who does Gabriela have dinner with?
She has dinner with her mom, dad, and two sisters.

2 What doesn't Gabriela always talk about at dinner?
....

3 What does Gabriela sometimes do on Saturday?
....

4 Who does Laura have dinner with?
....

5 What does Laura's brother often do at dinner?
....

3 WHAT A VACATION!

LANGUAGE REFERENCE

Simple Past of *to be*: Affirmative, Negative, *Yes/No* Questions, and Short Answers

Affirmative (+)	Negative (–)	*Yes/No* Questions (?)	Affirmative Short Answers (+)	Negative Short Answers (–)
I **was** at the museum. You **were** in Japan. He/She/It **was** in the historic center. We **were** in the country. They **were** in the swimming pool.	I **wasn't** at the beach. You **weren't** in the cafeteria. He/She/It **wasn't** in Mexico. We **weren't** at home. They **weren't** in the kitchen.	**Was** I at the beach? **Were** you at the hotel? **Was** he/she/it in Spain? **Were** we there? **Were** they in the restaurant?	Yes, I **was**. Yes, you **were**. Yes, he/she/it **was**. Yes, we **were**. Yes, they **were**.	No, I **wasn't**. No, you **weren't**. No, he/she/it **wasn't**. No, we **weren't**. No, they **weren't**.

There was/were: Affirmative, Negative, *Yes/No* Questions, and Short Answers

Affirmative (+)	Negative (–)	*Yes/No* Questions (?)	Affirmative Short Answers (+)	Negative Short Answers (–)
There was an interesting museum. **There were** a lot of tour guides.	**There wasn't** a swimming pool. **There weren't** beaches.	**Was there** an amusement park? **Were there** street markets?	Yes, **there was**. Yes, **there were**.	No, **there wasn't**. No, **there weren't**.

We use *There was* for singular nouns and *There were* for plural nouns.

On Vacation

amusement park
beach
camping
country
historic center
museum
sightseeing
street market

Facilities, People, and Activities

fishing
horseback riding
hotel room
kayaking
receptionist
safari
swimming pool
tour guide

VOCABULARY

1 Put the letters in the correct order and write the vacation words.

1 gamcpin camping
2 suumem ....
3 cebah ....
4 tmenuseam krpa ....
5 sithoric necter ....
6 treest ketram ....

2 Label images 1–6 with the vacation words from Exercise 1.

1

street market

2

....

3

....

4

....

5

....

6

....

3 Complete the chart with the words/phrases below.

- ~~fishing~~
- receptionist
- horseback riding
- safari
- hotel room
- swimming pool
- kayaking
- tour guide

People	Facilities	Activities
		fishing

4 Match 1–6 with a–f.

1 fishing b
2 kayaking ....
3 tour guide ....
4 receptionist ....
5 horseback riding ....
6 safari ....

A

B

C

D

E

F

GRAMMAR

1 Complete the sentences with *was*, *were*, *wasn't*, or *weren't*.

1 We ...were... in France. We weren't in Spain.
2 I was at the swimming pool this morning. I .... at the beach.
3 Ava and Mia .... at school yesterday. They were at home.
4 My sister wasn't in the kitchen. She .... in the yard.
5 I wasn't with Hana. I .... with Kokoro.
6 Jacob and I .... in the gymnasium. We were in the science lab.

2 Cross out the incorrect verbs and write the correct verbs.

Harry Anderson
To me
Subject Vacation

Hey, Ben

What a vacation! The town ~~were~~ was awesome! There was a lot of museums in the historic center and there were a really nice street market. The food were great and there was a lot of very good restaurants. There wasn't amusement parks near the town, but there were a very big swimming pool, and there was a skatepark, too. My parents, my brother, and I was all really happy!

Harry

3 Complete the mini dialogues with the correct simple past form of *to be*.

1 A ...Were... you in the hotel room?
B Yes, I ....
2 A .... Isabela in the clothing store?
B No, she ....
3 A .... Luis and Theo in the museum?
B No, they ....
4 A .... you and Riku in the amusement park?
B Yes, we ....

4 Complete the dialogue.

Ryan 1...Was... Ana downtown this morning?
Brenda No, she 2................................ . She 3................................ at the beach with her sister.
Ryan 4................................ her mom and dad downtown?
Brenda Yes, they 5................................ . They 6................................ at the street market. They love the fruit and vegetables there. And you? Where 7................................ you this morning?
Ryan I 8................................ at the swimming pool.
Brenda Nice!

READING

1 Look at the text and check (✓) the correct answers.

1 What is it?
◯ a blog post ◯ messages on social media

2 What is the text about?
◯ Lucas's family ◯ Lucas's vacation

Hey, Lucas, you weren't at Liam's birthday party on Saturday! Were you on vacation? 9:24

Hi, Samuel! Yes, we were – for two weeks. It was awesome! 😉 9:24

Cool! Were you in Spain? 9:25

No, we weren't. We were in France with my aunt and uncle in a big house. 9:25

Nice! Was there a swimming pool at the house? 9:26

No, there wasn't, but there was a beach near the house and it was great. My cousins and I were there every day, playing volleyball and swimming in the ocean. 9:26

Were there other things to do? 9:27

Wow, yes! Horseback riding, fishing, going to restaurants, but best of all, hanging out with my cousins! The local town was good, too. Nice parks (one with a skatepark), really good street markets, and even a bowling alley. There were a lot of museums, too, so Mom and Dad were happy! 9:27

Awesome! 9:28

2 Read the text and check (✓) the word/phrase that completes each sentence.

1 Last Saturday, Lucas was …
a at a birthday party. ◯ b in Spain. ◯ c in France. ✓

2 Lucas was on vacation for …
a three weeks. ◯ b two weeks. ◯ c a week. ◯

3 Lucas's favorite activity was …
a swimming. ◯ b horseback riding. ◯ c being with his cousins. ◯

4 The skatepark was …
a near the beach. ◯ b near the house. ◯ c in a park. ◯

5 Lucas's mom and dad like …
a museums. ◯ b bowling alleys. ◯ c skateparks. ◯

3 Write answers to the questions.

1 Was Lucas with Liam and Samuel last Saturday?
No, he wasn't. He was on vacation.

2 Was Lucas's vacation fun?
....

3 Was Lucas with his cousins' parents on vacation?
....

4 Was Lucas staying in a small hotel?
....

5 Were Lucas and his cousins in a swimming pool every day?
....

4 WE ALL HAVE A STORY

LANGUAGE REFERENCE

Simple Past of Regular Verbs

Verbs	Ending	Affirmative (+)	Negative (–)
Most verbs (for example, listen, play, walk, want)	Add *–ed*.	We **listened** to music. They **played** on the beach. She **walked** to school. I **wanted** a drink.	We **didn't listen**. They **didn't play**. She **didn't walk** to school. I **didn't want** a drink.
Verb ends in *–e* (for example, arrive, dance, like)	Add *–d*.	They **arrived** early. We **danced**. I **liked** the food.	They **didn't arrive** late. We **didn't dance**. I **didn't like** the food.
Verb ends in consonant + *–y* (for example, cry, fry, try)	Change *–y* to *–i* and add *–ed*.	She **cried.** I **fried** the onions. We **tried** to help.	She **didn't cry**. I **didn't fry** the onions. We **didn't try** to help.
Verb ends in consonant + vowel + consonant (for example, plan, stop)	Double the final consonant and add *–ed*.	They **planned** to go. He **stopped** swimming.	They **didn't plan** to go. He **didn't stop** swimming.

Simple Past of Irregular Verbs

Infinitive	Affirmative (+)	Negative (–)
go	I **went** to the swimming pool.	I **didn't go** to the park.
have	You **had** dark hair.	You **didn't have** blond hair.
read	He **read** the book last year.	He **didn't read** the book.
say	Ana **said**, "Good luck!"	Ana **didn't say** anything.
see	We **saw** Juliana's parents there.	We **didn't see** her parents.
take	They **took** some food with us.	They **didn't take** food with us

Story Verbs

arrive
decide
laugh
remember
rush
shout
tell
walk
want

Time Expressions

in the past
last week
now
one day
years ago
yesterday

VOCABULARY

1 Look at the images and circle the correct options.

1

He usually *shouts* / *arrives* home at five o'clock.

2

It's a beautiful day! They *decide* / *remember* to walk to school.

3

She always *walks* / *wants* to go swimming.

4

He's late again. He *rushes* / *shouts* to his class.

5

They *laugh* / *rush* a lot when they watch his movies.

6

They're sleeping. Please don't *tell* / *shout*!

2 Match 1–5 with a–e.

1 My grandpa tells ..d..
2 Remember ....
3 Please, don't shout ....
4 We often walk ....
5 I always arrive ....

a to say "Happy Birthday" to Luisa!
b to school.
c at school at 8:30.
d us great stories.
e at your brother!

3 Complete the sentences with the words below.

• ago • day • last • ~~now~~ • past • yesterday

1 I'm doing my homework ....now.... .
2 In the ...., children often walked to school.
3 Three years ...., I started playing basketball.
4 .... week, I decided to go horseback riding.
5 We arrived in Spain ....
6 One ...., he decided to visit his sister.

4 Put the words in the correct order.

1 a cell / phone now / people / most / young / have
Most young people have a cell phone now.
2 the / danced to / in / people / this music / past
....
3 United States / ago / we / three / arrived / weeks / in the
....
4 day, he / one / take / to town / decided to / the bus
....
5 played / in the / yesterday / soccer / park / I
....
6 Saturday / skatepark / last / to / we / walked / the
....

GRAMMAR

1 Write the simple past form of regular verbs 1–8.

1 decide ......decided......
2 listen ....
3 cry ....
4 like ....
5 laugh ....
6 plan ....
7 try ....
8 want ....

2 Complete the sentences with the correct simple past form.

1 Theo ......kicked...... (kick) the ball to me.
2 We .... (dance) for three hours!
3 I liked all the food, but I .... (love) the pizza!
4 He .... (fry) the chicken.
5 Akari .... (try) to help him.
6 They .... (stop) running.

3 Complete the sentences with the correct simple past form of the irregular verbs below.

• go • have • ~~read~~ • say • see • take

1 I ......read...... a really good book last month.
2 Helena and I .... a great movie on Saturday.
3 We .... to France on vacation.
4 I .... lunch with Noah in the cafeteria.
5 The man .... , "Can I help you?"
6 I .... a bus to the stadium.

4 Complete the sentences with the correct negative simple past form of the verbs. Then look at the images and write affirmative sentences.

1 I ...didn't have... (not have) cereal for breakfast this morning.
2 Vitoria .... (not go) to the bowling alley.
3 We .... (not laugh) at the story.
4 I .... (not read) that book at home.
5 The teacher .... (not shout) at Juan.
6 You .... (not do) your math homework.

1

.........I had eggs.........
....

2

....
....

3

....
....

4

....
....

5

....
....

6

....
....

READING

1 Look at the text and check (✓) the correct answers.

1 What is it?
- ◯ an email
- ◯ an article
- ◯ a story

2 The author thinks ...
- ◯ stories are not important.
- ◯ we can learn from stories.
- ◯ stories are boring.

Why are stories so important?

Stories ...

... expand our imagination!

In stories, we meet people we don't know. These people are often very different from us. Sometimes they are even fantastical. We go to other countries, and we learn about new cultures and situations. We can imagine lives and places that are different from ours. This expands our imagination.

... teach us how to be good!

Some stories teach us something. At the end of the story, the bad people suffer, and the good people win. These stories can inspire us. We learn how to treat other people well.

... give us empathy!

Some people say this is the most important thing about stories. Stories make us experience other people's problems, and we feel their emotions. We understand how other people feel, and we understand why they do things. Some people even say that children who read a lot of stories have more empathy. They have better connections with other people.

... are fun!

Finally, stories are fun. We read stories until the end because we want to know what happens. We enjoy them!

2 Read the text and write *T* (true) or *F* (false) next to the statements.

1 In stories, we only read about people who are the same as us. F
2 We often experience new things in stories. ....
3 Stories help us to be imaginative. ....
4 Stories never teach us to be good people. ....
5 Stories help us to understand other people's emotions. ....

3 Complete the sentences with words from the text.

1 People in stories aren't always real. They can be fantastical.
2 In stories we can experience different .... that show us different ways of life.
3 Some stories can teach us how to .... other people well.
4 Children who read a lot of stories understand how other people ....
5 We read all of a story because we want to know what happens at the ....

5 INCREDIBLE JOURNEYS

LANGUAGE REFERENCE

Simple Past of Regular and Irregular Verbs: Questions and Answers

Yes/No Questions (?)	Short Answers
Did I **tell** you?	Yes, I **did**. / No, I **didn't**.
Did you **drive** to the beach?	Yes, you **did**. / No, you **didn't**.
Did he/she/it **arrive**?	Yes, he/she/it **did**. / No, he/she/it **didn't**.
Did we **eat** there?	Yes, we **did**. / No, we **didn't**.
Did they **get off** the train?	Yes, they **did**. / No, they **didn't**.
***Wh–* Questions (?)**	**Answers**
Where did you **get on** the bus?	At the station.
How did she **get** there?	She walked.
When did they **go** home?	At nine o'clock.

We use the infinitive form of the verb in questions.

Could for Ability in the Past

Affirmative (+)	Negative (–)	*Yes/No* Questions (?)	Short Answers
I **could ride** a bike at that age.	I **couldn't drive** a car then.	**Could** I **walk** at that age?	Yes, I **could**. / No, I **couldn't**.
You **could kick** a ball when you were two.	You **couldn't speak** English.	**Could** you **ski**?	Yes, you **could**. / No, you **couldn't**.
He/She/It **could run** fast.	He/She/It **couldn't throw**.	**Could** he/she/it **swim**?	Yes, he/she/it **could**. / No, he/she/it **couldn't**.
We **could take** the bus to the campground.	We **couldn't remember** her name.	**Could** we **get off** the train there?	Yes, we **could**. / No, we **couldn't**.
They **could have** dinner in a restaurant.	They **couldn't find** a grocery store.	**Could** they **surf**?	Yes, they **could**. / No, they **couldn't**.

We use *could* and *couldn't* to talk about ability in the past.

Transportation

airplane
boat
car
ferry
motorcycle
scooter
subway
taxi
van

Transportation Verbs

board (an airplane)
drive (a car)
get off (the train)
get on / take (the train)
miss (the bus)
ride (a bike)
wait for (the bus)

VOCABULARY

1 Find eight transportation words.

Z	A	I	R	P	L	A	N	E	B	V
O	J	I	S	Q	U	P	W	Q	S	X
O	D	H	U	B	Y	S	D	S	F	F
J	M	O	T	O	R	C	Y	C	L	E
T	R	H	A	A	Y	G	D	O	K	R
W	T	M	X	T	T	D	S	O	D	R
U	X	V	I	F	G	U	G	T	U	Y
S	U	B	W	A	Y	G	R	E	I	T
Y	B	S	D	I	Y	C	A	R	A	S

2 Label images 1–6 with the words below.

• airplane • ferry • motorcycle • ~~scooter~~ • subway • van

1 

scooter

2 

....

3 

....

4 

....

5 

....

6 

....

3 Put the letters in the correct order and complete the sentences.

1 We ..boarded.. (baedrod) the airplane at 9:30 a.m.
2 Did you .... (kaet) the bus to the mall?
3 We were late and .... (simsde) the train!
4 A lot of people .... (rived) their children to school.
5 Rafael is only three years old, but he can .... (deri) a bike.
6 We .... (detiwa) for the bus for an hour.
7 I usually............................ (tge fof) the train at Oxford.

4 Match 1–5 with a–e.

1 I'm waiting ..d..
2 She drives ....
3 Get ....
4 I ride ....
5 They boarded ....

a a blue car.
b my bike to school.
c the airplane in New York.
d for the bus.
e on the next train.

GRAMMAR

1 Complete the mini dialogues with one or two words.

1 A ....Did.... you add salt to the beans?
B No, I ....

2 A .... they remember the food?
B Yes, they ....

3 A .... Bruno miss the ferry?
B Yes, he ....

4 A .... Marcela go?
B She went to Spain.

5 A .... James and William arrive?
B They arrived yesterday.

2 Put the words in the correct order.

1 food / you / healthy / eat / did
........Did you eat healthy food?........

2 to / the / did / walk / he / bowling alley
....

3 she / fish / how / did / the / cook
....

4 did / they / where / movie / watch / the
....

5 you / did / how / school / get / to
....

6 Takumi / go / did / when / bed / to
....

3 Complete the dialogue with *could* or *couldn't*.

Mariana [1]....Could.... you do your math homework last night?

Leticia I [2].................... do the first three questions, they were easy, but I [3].................... do questions 4 and 5. I didn't understand them.

Mariana All the questions were too difficult for me. I [4].................... do one question.

Leticia Why [5].................... you ask your dad to help you? He's good at math.

Mariana He wasn't at home last night. I [6].................... ask him.

4 Complete the sentences. Use *could* or *couldn't* and the verbs below.

~~drive~~ • go • ride • speak • take • wear

1 I ....couldn't drive.... a car when I was in France. (–)
2 We .... horseback riding last weekend. (–)
3 At my first school, I .... sneakers and jeans. (+)
4 My mom .... French and English when she was ten. (+)
5 Raquel .... her bike after her accident. (–)
6 When we lived in Recife we .... the subway to school. (+)

READING

1 Look at the text and check (✓) the correct answers.

1 What is it?
- ◯ a newspaper article
- ◯ information on an educational website
- ◯ messages on social media

2 What is it about?
- ◯ the climate
- ◯ the good things about traveling by boat
- ◯ a long boat trip by a young girl

HOME | **DAILY LESSONS** | SUPPORT

An Incredible Journey

Part of **Geography**

In the summer of 2019, a 16-year-old girl named Greta Thunberg traveled on a boat from the UK to New York. The trip was more than 4,800 kilometers and took 15 days.

Why did Greta Thunberg go to New York?

She wanted to go to an important conference there on climate change.

Why did she travel by boat?

Greta didn't want to travel by airplane because airplanes are one of the causes of climate change.

When did she arrive in New York?

Greta arrived in New York on August 28.

Did she travel with friends or family?

Her dad traveled with her.

Did she enjoy the trip?

Yes! Greta couldn't take a shower – there wasn't a bathroom or even a toilet on the boat, and there wasn't a kitchen or a bedroom, but she liked being on the boat.

When Greta arrived in New York, hundreds of people came to meet her.

2 Read the text and write *T* (true) or *F* (false) next to the statements.

1 Greta's trip started in New York. F
2 Greta was on the boat for 15 days. ....
3 She was on vacation. ....
4 One member of her family was with her on the boat. ....
5 Greta took a lot of showers on the boat. ....
6 Greta didn't enjoy the trip. ....

3 Write answers to the questions.

1 What time of year was the trip?
It was summer.

2 How old was Greta when the trip started?
....

3 What distance did the boat travel?
....

4 What was the conference in New York about?
....

5 What facilities didn't the boat have?
....

6 How many people came to meet Greta when she arrived in New York?
....

6 HEROES MAKE A DIFFERENCE

LANGUAGE REFERENCE

Past Progressive: Affirmative and Negative

Affirmative (+)	Negative (–)
I **was watching** a movie.	I **wasn't wearing** a coat.
You **were driving**.	You **weren't dancing**.
He/She/It **was running**.	He/She/It **wasn't swimming**.
We **were having** breakfast.	We **weren't playing** basketball.
They **were getting off** the train.	They **weren't laughing**.

Past Progressive: Questions and Answers

Yes/No Questions (?)	Short Answers
Was I **riding** a bike?	Yes, I **was**. / No, I **wasn't**.
Were you **waiting** for the bus?	Yes, you **were**. / No, you **weren't**.
Was he/she/it **walking**?	Yes, he/she/it **was**. / No, he/she/it **wasn't**.
Were we **playing** soccer?	Yes, we **were**. / No, we **weren't**.
Were they **listening** to music?	Yes, they **were**. / No, they **weren't**.
***Wh–* Questions (?)**	**Answers**
What were you **doing**?	I **was hanging out** with my friends.
Why was he **waiting**?	He **was waiting** for Bruna to arrive.
Where were they **going**?	They **were going** to the cafeteria.

Personality Adjectives

amazing
boring
brave
friendly
funny
kind
lazy
smart
strong

Feelings

angry
bored
excited
happy
sad
surprised
tired
worried

VOCABULARY

1 Find six adjectives.

aopw(amazing)toptyusmartbuqaklbravecopterstrongmiklopkindertyufriendlyckling

1 amazing
2 ....
3 ....
4 ....
5 ....
6 ....

2 Complete the sentences and the crossword with the correct personality adjectives.

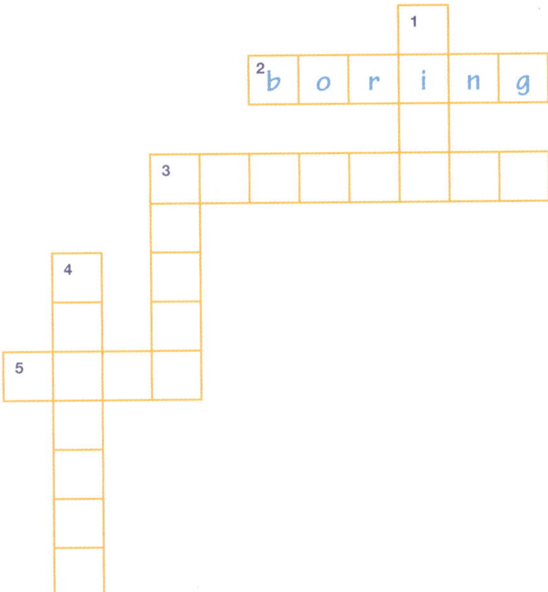

Across

2 He never says anything interesting. He's very boring.
3 My brother is really nice, and he speaks to everyone. He's very ....
5 Rafaela never does any exercise. She's ....

Down

1 My dad always helps people. He's very ....
3 I laugh a lot when I'm with Bruna. She's very ....
4 Wonder Woman is strong and smart, and she can fly! She's ....

3 Circle the correct options.

1 I walked fifteen kilometers this morning, and now I'm *angry* / (*tired*)
2 There was a cat in our classroom this morning. The teacher was very *surprised* / *bored*!
3 My dad is *tired* / *worried* because we missed the train.
4 We're going on vacation! I'm really *angry* / *excited*!
5 We do the same thing every day, and I'm *bored* / *excited*.
6 I'm *angry* / *happy* when I hang out with my friends.

4 Put the letters in the correct order and write the feelings. Then complete sentences a–e.

1 robde bored
2 itder ....
3 payph ....
4 sda ....
5 nragy ....

a This class is not interesting. I'm bored!
b Sofia didn't do her homework. Her teacher was .... and shouted at her.
c My cousin's best friend didn't come to his birthday party. He was .... and cried.
d I'm going to bed now. I'm very ....
e Hey, it's my birthday! I'm so ....!

GRAMMAR

1 Complete the sentences with *was* or *were*.

1 We ....were.......... boarding the plane.
2 Emma .... talking to Charlotte.
3 I .... having my breakfast.
4 My friends .... playing basketball.
5 You .... cooking in the kitchen.
6 Daniel .... speaking on his cell phone.

2 Complete the sentences with the correct past progressive form of the verbs.

1 Beatriz ....was wearing.......... (wear) her school uniform. (+)
2 Elijah and I .... (watch) a movie. (+)
3 You .... (listen) to me. (–)
4 My sister .... (drive) the car. (+)
5 I .... (shout) at you! (–)
6 We .... (eat) junk food. (–)

3 Put the words in the correct order to make questions.

1 black / mom / was / a / jacket / wearing / your
..........Was your mom wearing a black jacket?..........
2 the world / his / were / parents / around / traveling
....?
3 your / you / were / doing / homework
....?
4 was / brother / with Liam / swimming / your
....?
5 I / was / toward / walking / school
....?

4 Complete the mini dialogues with the correct words.

1 A I saw you yesterday morning. ....Were.......... you waiting for a bus?
B Yes, I .... I was going home.
2 A .... Olivia talking to Carla at the party?
B No, she .... She was talking to Ana.
3 A .... Samuel doing in the park?
B He was playing soccer.
4 A .... Lucas and Miguel going last night?
B They were going to the bowling alley.
5 A .... Amanda shouting?
B She was angry with Samuel.

READING

1 **Look at the text and check (✓) the correct answers.**

1 What is it?
- ◯ information about cats
- ◯ a story about a cat
- ◯ a story about a lot of cats

2 The author's name is ...
- ◯ Lulu.
- ◯ Luisa.
- ◯ David.

We are so happy to have our cat Lulu home! Last Saturday, Lulu didn't come inside to eat her dinner, and we didn't see her the next day. My mom and I were getting really worried. We looked in the park and in people's yards, but we couldn't find her anywhere. On Sunday evening I was looking out into the street from my bedroom and I saw Lulu! She was in a tree, about fifteen meters up. I was so surprised. Mom and I went into the street and shouted "Lulu!," but she didn't come down. We put her favorite food under the tree, but she didn't come down. We don't know why, but she couldn't move. We were really sad.

On Tuesday Lulu was still in the tree. My mom decided to post a message on Facebook and ask for help. A kind man named David read the message. He works with trees and he rushed to our house in his van. He used his equipment to get to Lulu and bring her down, and now she is home with us again. What a hero!

Luisa, 13

2 **Read the text and write *T* (true) or *F* (false) next to the statements.**

1 Lulu is not in the tree now. T
2 Luisa and her mom looked for Lulu in people's houses. ....
3 Lulu was in the tree for more than three days. ....
4 Lulu came down the tree when she saw her favorite food. ....
5 David saw the post about Lulu. ....
6 David shouted the cat's name, and she came down. ....

3 **Write answers to the questions.**

1 Which day did Luisa's cat not eat her dinner for the first time?
She didn't eat her dinner for the first time on Saturday.
2 How were Luisa and her mom feeling during the day on Sunday?
....
3 What was Luisa doing when she saw Lulu?
....
4 What did Luisa and her mom put under the tree?
....
5 What did Luisa's mom do on Tuesday?
....
6 What is David's job?
....

7

GREAT IDEAS

LANGUAGE REFERENCE

Past Progressive and Simple Past

when	I **was walking** down Elm Street **when** I **saw** her.
while	I **learned** to cook **while** I **was living** in Spain. **While** we **were watching** a movie, Dad **was making** dinner.

We use *while* + past progressive for past actions in progress.
We use *when* + simple past for past events at a particular moment.

Possessive Pronouns

Possessive Pronouns		
mine	**Whose** sweatshirt is this?	It's my sweatshirt. It's **mine**.
yours	**Whose** headphones are these?	They're your headphones. They're **yours**.
his	**Whose** jacket is this?	It's my brother's. It's **his**.
hers	**Whose** pen is this?	It's my mom's. It's **hers**.
ours	**Whose** shoes are these?	They're our shoes. They're **ours**.
theirs	**Whose** motorcycle is this?	It's their motorcycle. It's **theirs**.

Innovation verbs

become
build
create
discover
fly
invent
start
take
use

Technology

battery
headphones
keyboard
printer
screen
tablet

VOCABULARY

1 Circle the correct options.

1 In 1783, two Frenchmen *flew* / *started* in a hot air balloon in Paris.
2 Scientists *discovered* / *built* two planets outside the solar system in 1992.
3 In 2008, Barack Obama *created* / *became* the first African American president of the United States.
4 Russell Kirsch *took* / *discovered* the first digital photograph in 1957.
5 Sir Tim Berners-Lee *invented* / *became* the World Wide Web in 1989.
6 In the 1950s, a lot of young people *created* / *started* to wear jeans.

2 Put the letters in the correct order and complete the sentences.

1 Mary Anning ...discovered... (sidceroved) the fossils of many dinosaurs.
2 Ralph Baer .... (acerted) the first video game.
3 The company .... (sued) old sweatshirts and T-shirts to make new clothes.
4 Baron Karl von Drais .... (lubit) the first bicycle in 1817.
5 Nancy Johnson .... (vennited) the first ice cream maker in 1843.
6 Janet Jagan .... (ebcema) the first American woman to be president of a country.

3 Label images 1–6 with the words below.

• battery • ~~keyboard~~ • printer • headphones • tablet • screen

1 
...keyboard...

2 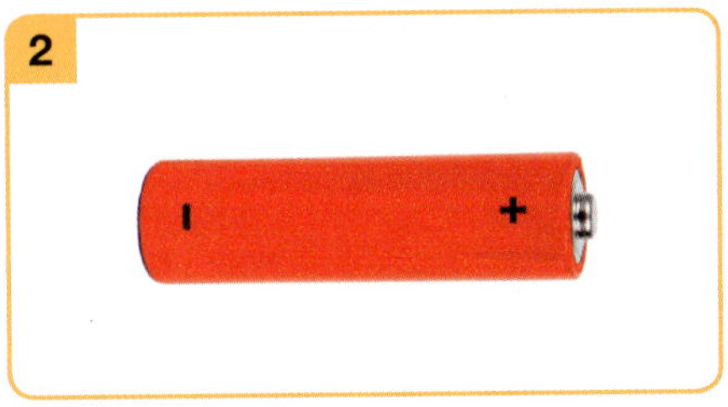
....

3 
....

4 
....

5 
....

6 
....

4 Circle the correct options.

1 This is a small computer. *screen / printer / tablet*
2 You look at this part of a cell phone, computer, or TV. *screen / keyboard / tablet*
3 You put these on your ears to listen to music. *battery / headphones / keyboard*
4 This object gives electricity to cars, cell phones, and radios. *printer / battery / screen*
5 One of the parts of a computer with letters on it. *keyboard / tablet / battery*
6 You use this to make a lot of copies of a document. *tablet / headphones / printer*

GRAMMAR

1 **Complete the sentences with the correct past progressive form of the verbs.**

1 Paulo was doing his homework while I ....was taking.......... (take) a shower.
2 While we .... (ride) our bikes, you were waiting for a bus.
3 Dad .... (fry) the vegetables while I was mixing the eggs.
4 Alex and Theo .... (play) a video game while I was having breakfast.
5 While my mom was studying to become a doctor, my dad .... (work) as a teacher.
6 While you were getting off the train, I .... (get on) the train!

2 **Circle the correct options.**

1 We were playing volleyball in the park when we *were seeing* / *saw* him.
2 I *was walking* / *walked* to school when I remembered it was Enzo's birthday.
3 He saw the accident while he *drove* / *was driving* to work.
4 When Russell Kirsch *took* / *was taking* the first digital photograph he was making images for his wife.
5 I was reading my book when I *heard* / *was hearing* a shout from the kitchen.
6 When I saw Camila she *was rushing* / *rushed* for the train.

3 **Cross out the incorrect words and write the correct words.**

1 A Whose tablet is this?
B It's ~~my~~. ....mine..........
2 The man stopped us and looked in ours bags. ....
3 They know our address, but we don't know their. ....
4 This is mine cell phone. That one is Yuto's. ....
5 That's Victor's pizza! Your has more cheese on it. ....
6 Those aren't Hana's earphones. Her are black. ....

4 **Complete the sentences with the correct possessive pronouns.**

1 It's your tablet. It's ....yours.......... .
2 They're Ana's jeans. They're ....
3 It's our car. It's ....
4 They're Felipe's headphones. They're ....
5 That's my bike. That's ....
6 That's my parents' computer. That's ....

READING

1 Look at the text and check (✓) the correct answers.

1 What is it?
- ◯ an email
- ◯ a blog post
- ◯ a webpage

2 What is it about?
- ◯ ice skating in winter
- ◯ winter in Maine, USA
- ◯ a boy who invented something

www.thehistoryofinventions.com

FAMOUS INVENTORS ART FOOD & DRINK **CLOTHES** THE HOME

It was around 1870, and an American boy named Chester Greenwood was doing his favorite thing, ice skating, when his ears started to hurt. They were so cold. He lived in Maine, in the United States, and in winter it was very cold. Chester put his hands over his cold ears, but then it was difficult to skate. He tried covering his head with a hat, but his ears were still cold, and they still hurt!

Then Chester had an idea. He made two circular covers for his ears and connected the covers with a fine piece of metal. He then put his invention on his head. He created the world's first earmuffs! He could now skate, and his ears were warm! His friends wanted earmuffs for their cold ears, and he made some for them. A few years later, Chester built a factory to make earmuffs. By 1883, his factory was making 50,000 every year!

2 Read the text and write *T* (true) or *F* (false) next to the statements.

1 Chester Greenwood didn't like ice skating. F
2 Winters weren't cold in the place where he lived. ....
3 Chester's ears were very cold while he was skating. ....
4 He invented something to keep his ears warm. ....
5 Chester's friends didn't like his invention. ....
6 He built an earmuffs factory. ....

3 Write answers to the questions.

1 Where did Chester live?
He lived in Maine, in the United States.

2 What did Chester like doing best?
....

3 What happened when Chester went skating?
....

4 How did he connect the two circular covers?
....

5 What did his friends want?
....

6 How many earmuffs did Chester's factory make in 1883?
....

8 OUR NATURAL WORLD

LANGUAGE REFERENCE

Verbs to Express Likes, Wants, and Needs

Hate*, *Like*, *Love*, *Need*, and *Want	
Simple Present	**Simple Past**
I **hate to** see all the trash. You **like to** walk by the lake. He/She **loves to** watch the birds. We **need to** take our bottles home. They **want to** swim in the ocean.	I **hated to** see all the cars in the town. You **liked to** take photos of the flowers. He/She **loved to** climb in the hills. We **needed to** stop using plastic bags. They **wanted to** ride their bikes to the coast.

Connectors

After*, *And*, *Before*, *But*, *However*, and *So	
Addition	There are a lot of birds **and** there are some beautiful flowers.
Opposition	It's very nice by the coast, **but** it's cold. It's easy to clean the beaches. **However**, the ocean is more difficult.
Consequence	It was snowy, **so** I wore my coat and hat.
Time	Have your lunch **before** you go to the beach. **After** the stormy weather yesterday, we're enjoying the sun today.

Nature

birds
coast
fields
flowers
grass
hill
lake
ocean
trees
village

The Weather

cloudy
foggy
rainy
snowy
stormy
sunny
windy

VOCABULARY

1 Complete the nature words.

1 We climbed up the h~~ill~~............
2 Please don't walk on the g............
3 My sister likes to swim in the l............, but I prefer to swim in the o............
4 I can hear a lot of b............ singing!
5 They live in a small v............
6 My aunt has beautiful red and yellow f............ in her yard.

2 Label images 1–5 with the words below.

• ~~birds~~ • coast • flowers • fields • trees

1

............birds............

2

....

3

....

4

....

5

....

3 Match sentences 1–6 with images a–f.

What was the weather like?

1 It was stormy all night. ....d....
2 It was very rainy. ....
3 It was nice and sunny. ....
4 It was foggy all day. ....
5 It was snowy all winter. ....
6 It was cloudy. ....

A

D

B

E

C

F

4 Circle the correct options.

1 On *windy* / *(rainy)* days, there's water everywhere.
2 Why aren't you wearing your new T-shirt? It's a nice *rainy* / *sunny* day.
3 It's a beautiful *rainy* / *snowy* day – everything is white.
4 It's so *cloudy* / *windy*! Look at the trees moving!
5 It was really *sunny* / *foggy* this morning – I couldn't see anything in front of me.

GRAMMAR

1 Put the words in the correct order.

1 you / to / bed / to / need / go

You need to go to bed.

2 photos / fish in / I / to / the ocean / like / take / of

....

3 hate / to / we / see / plastic in / all the / the water

....

4 we / go / beach / horseback / want / to / on the / riding

....

5 street market / loves / Sakura / buy / to / flowers / at the

....

2 Look at the words and images. Use the prompts to write sentences.

1 My grandma / love / see

My grandma loves to see flowers.

2 Luis / like / hang out with

....

3 We / need / do

....

4 I / want / plant

....

5 My cousin / love / run

....

6 My dad / hate / see

....

3 Circle the correct options.

1 The ocean is perfect. It's clean *so* / *and* the water's warm.
2 You can swim in the lake, *but* / *and* the water's very cold.
3 It was a sunny day, *so* / *but* we went for a walk.
4 The coast is nice in the winter. *However,* / *So* it's awesome in the summer.
5 Ask Gabriel *after* / *before* you take his bike to the park!

4 Complete the sentences with the words below.

• after • and • ~~before~~ • but • so

1 Wash your hands before you start cooking.
2 Carolina is smart, ... she's very lazy.
3 It was windy and rainy, ... we stayed at home.
4 .... doing a lot of exercise, I'm very hungry.
5 The historic center is beautiful, ... it's very interesting.

READING

1 Look at the text and check (✓) the correct answers.

1 Where is it from?
- ◯ a website
- ◯ a magazine
- ◯ a book

2 What is it about?
- ◯ trash in the ocean
- ◯ a vacation at the beach
- ◯ a new invention

THE OCEAN CLEAN-UP

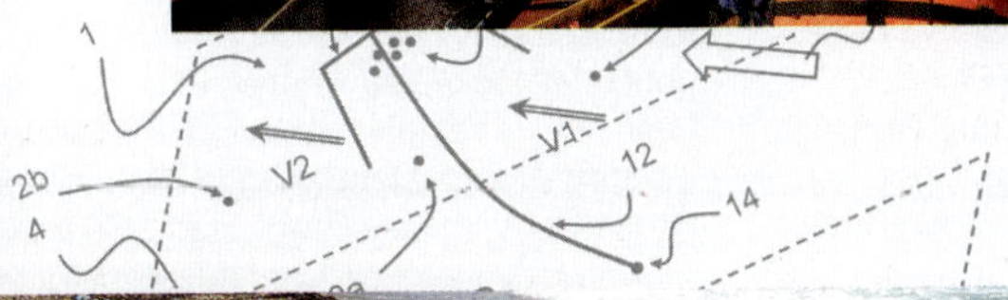

One day, a 16-year-old Dutch boy named Boyan Slat was swimming in the Mediterranean Sea when he saw a lot of plastic. In fact, he saw more plastic bags than fish! Boyan was very worried. He hated to see so much trash in the water. He started a project at school to study plastic pollution. He wanted to know why it was so difficult to clean up plastic from the ocean.

When Boyan was 17, he invented an object for cleaning the oceans. The object looks like a very long arm. The arm moves over the top of the water. As it moves, it collects the plastic that is on top of the water. The fish are OK: they swim under it! This arm collects big and small pieces of plastic. It can even clean up pieces as small as 1 millimeter. Every six weeks, boats take the plastic to a place where people can recycle it.

Boyan Slat says he wants to clean up 90% of the plastic from the top of the oceans.

2 Read the text and complete the sentences. Use phrases in the text.

1 While Boyan Slat was swimming, he saw ......a lot of plastic...... .
2 He invented an object .... the oceans.
3 He invented the object when he .... years old.
4 The object he invented looks like ....
5 The fish are safe because they .... it.

3 Write answers to the questions.

1 Where was Boyan Slat swimming when he saw the plastic?
......He was swimming in the Mediterranean Sea......

2 How did he feel when he saw so much plastic?
....

3 What did he start to study at school?
....

4 How does the arm collect the plastic?
....

5 How often do boats come to take the plastic for recycling?
....

Thanks and Acknowledgements

We would like to thank the following people for their invaluable contribution to the series:

Ruth Atkinson, Sue Andre Costello, Lauren Fenton, Justine Gesell, Tom Hadland, Cara Norris, Maria Toth, Kate Woodford and Liz Walter.

The authors and editors would like to thank all the teachers who have contributed to the development of the course:

Geysla Lopes de Alencar, Priscila Araújo, David Williams Mocock de Araújo, Leticia da Silva Azevedo, Francisco Evangelista Ferreira Batista, Luiz Fernando Carmo, Thiago Silva Campos, Cintia Castilho, Mônica Egydio, Érica Fernandes, Viviane Azevêdo de Freitas, Marco Giovanni, Rodolfo de Aro da Rocha Keizer, Vanessa Leroy, Bruno Fernandes de Lima, Allana Tavares Maciel, Jonadab Mansur, Rogério dos Santos Melo, Carlos Ubiratã Gois de Menezes, Aryanne Moreira, Joelba Geane da Silva, Vanessa Silva Pereira, Daniela Costa Pinheiro, Isa de França Vasconcelos, Eliana Perrucci Vergani, Geraldo Vieira, Whebston Mozart.

The authors and publishers acknowledge the following sources of copyright material and are grateful for the permissions granted. While every effort has been made, it has not always been possible to identify the sources of all the material used, or to trace all copyright holders. If any omissions are brought to our notice, we will be happy to include the appropriate acknowledgements on reprinting and in the next update to the digital edition, as applicable.

Key: R = Review, U = Unit, W = Welcome

Student's Book

Photography

The following images are sourced from Getty Images.

UW: IconicBestiary/iStock/Getty Images Plus; dikobraziy/iStock/Getty Images Plus; frimages/iStock/Getty Images Plus; Thurtell/E+; bortonia/DigitalVision; Irina_Strelnikova/iStock/Getty Images Plus; **U1**: monkeybusinessimages/iStock/Getty Images Plus; Welcome to buy my photos/Moment; John Kieffer/Photolibrary; Russelltatedotcom/DigitalVision; urbancow/E+; HRAUN/E+; Walter Zerla; Mladen Antonov/AFP; Yulia Melnyk/iStock/Getty Images Plus; SDI Productions/iStock/Getty Images Plus; Csondy/E+; Turgay Malikli/iStock/Getty Images Plus; Oleksandr Yashnyi/iStock/Getty Images Plus; Zsolt Hlinka/Moment; JohnnyGreig/E+; Mathias Rhode/iStock/Getty Images Plus; Gideon Mendel/Corbis Historical; Zhang Peng/LightRocket; Barbulat/iStock/Getty Images Plus; TongSur/DigitalVision Vectors; Jasmin Merdan/Moment; Pollyana Ventura/iStock/Getty Images Plus; Ormuzd Alves/LatinContent WO; Pollyana Ventura/E+; FerreiraSilva/iStock Editorial/Getty Images Plus; Gil Vicente Xaxas/iStock/Getty Images Plus; Userba9fe9ab_931/iStock/Getty Images Plus; Maskot; Dobrila Vignjevic/iStock/Getty Images Plus; Goodshoot; Eric Raptosh Photography; yayayoyo/iStock/Getty Images Plus; Vect0r0vich/iStock/Getty Images Plus; **U2**: Rawpixel Ltd/iStock/Getty Images Plus; Silmairel/iStock/Getty Images Plus; sveta_zarzamora/iStock/Getty Images Plus; RedHelga/E+; Yevgen Romanenko/Moment; nazar_ab/iStock/Getty Images Plus; Basilios1/E+; Ekachai Lohacamonchai/EyeEm; Boonchuay1970/iStock/Getty Images Plus; Javier Zayas Photography/Moment; EugeneTomeev/iStock/Getty Images Plus; golubovy/iStock/Getty Images Plus; Suparat Malipoom/EyeEm; Василий Авраменко/iStock/Getty Images Plus; Brian Macdonald/DigitalVision; TheCrimsonMonkey/E+; GI15702993/iStock/Getty Images Plus; Steven Morris Photography/Photolibrary; ullstein bild; pop_jop/DigitalVision Vectors; Christian Science Monitor; tkacchuk/iStock/Getty Images Plus; Maximilian Stock Ltd/Photolibrary; mariusFM77/E+; NickS/E+; LongHa2006/E+; serezniy/iStock/Getty Images Plus; Stanislav Sablin/iStock/Getty Images Plus; Phaelnogueira/iStock/Getty Images Plus; Victor Coscaron/EyeEm; Luxy; 7Crafts/iStock/Getty Images Plus; eliflamra/iStock/Getty Images Plus; Eisenhut and Mayer Wien/Photolibrary/Getty Images Plus; Thomas J Peterson/Photographer's Choice/Getty Images Plus; monkeybusinessimages/iStock/Getty Images Plus; Tamara Staples/The Image Bank; Aleksandr Filinkov/iStock/Getty Images Plus; Sjo/E+; cveltri/iStock Unreleased; undefined undefined/iStock/Getty Images Plus; AdShooter/E+; Photosiber/iStock/Getty Images Plus; Foodcollection; dirkr/E+; OksanaOO/iStock/Getty Images Plus; FARBAI/iStock/Getty Images Plus; Panptys/iStock/Getty Images Plus; **R1**: demaerre/iStock/Getty Images Plus; Barry Kusuma/Photolibrary; Jacobs Stock Photography Ltd/DigitalVision; International Rescue/The Image Bank; gaelgogo/iStock/Getty Images Plus; iuliia_n/iStock/Getty Images Plus; lenazap/iStock/Getty Images Plus; Seijiroooooooooo/iStock/Getty Images Plus; demaerre/iStock/Getty Images Plus; Barry Kusuma/Photolibrary; OksanaOO/iStock/Getty Images Plus; FARBAI/iStock/Getty Images Plus; Panptys/iStock/Getty Images Plus; **U3**: David De Lossy/DigitalVision; Chatree Petjan/EyeEm; Nastco/iStock/Getty Images Plus; Prashant Menon/500px; Alan Schein/The Image Bank; Antonel/iStock/Getty Images Plus; Karina Vera/EyeEm; Macis Alex/500px; Sol de Zuasnabar Brebbia/Moment; Ma yichao/Moment; petekarici/E+; lushik/DigitalVision Vectors; greyj/iStock/Getty Images Plus; enjoynz/DigitalVision Vectors; -VICTOR-/DigitalVision Vectors; vectorsmarket/iStock/Getty Images Plus; dikobraziy/iStock/Getty Images Plus; Vladyslav Bobuskyi/iStock/Getty Images Plus; MaksimYremenko/iStock/Getty Images Plus; Kubkoo/iStock/Getty Images Plus; kiszon pascal/Moment; Sir Francis Canker Photography/Moment; Peter Adams/The Image Bank Unreleased; Ricardo Lima/Moment; Egeris/iStock/Getty Images Plus; Atlantide Phototravel/The Image Bank Unreleased; PhotoTalk/E+; Ghislain & Marie David de Lossy/The Image Bank; Nikada/E+; Chad Wright Photography/Moment; Westend61; SolStock/E+; MoMo Productions/DigitalVision; Pierre-Yves Babelon/Moment; ctrlaplus1/iStock/Getty Images Plus; Cyndi Monaghan/Moment ; Martin Child; bgblue/DigitalVision Vectors; xavierarnau/E+; Image Source; lucentius/E+; R.Tsubin/Moment; Roger Weber/Photodisc; **U4**: Nancy Honey/The Image Bank/Getty Images Plus; Design Pics/Colleen Cahill; iStockphoto/Getty Images; L-TOP/iStock/Getty Images Plus; Mint Images/Mint Images RF; cenkerdem/DigitalVision Vectors; piyaset/iStock/Getty Images Plus; Roman Bykhalets/iStock/Getty Images Plus; duckycards/E+; colematt/iStock/Getty Images Plus; stockcam/E+; Klaus Vedfelt/DigitalVision; Lilanakani/iStock/Getty Images Plus; Olga Kurbatova/iStock/Getty Images Plus; Jolygon/iStock/Getty Images Plus; Antonio_Diaz/iStock/Getty Images Plus; denkcreative/DigitalVision Vectors; thipjang/Moment; duncan1890/DigitalVision Vectors; David Fletcher/Moment Open; Heritage Images/Hulton Archive; Archive Holdings Inc./Archive Photos; Lambert/Fototrove; dial-a-view/iStock/Getty Images Plus; jemastock/iStock/Getty Images Plus; Nick David/Stone; **R2**: suefeldberg/iStock/Getty Images Plus; Zephyr18/iStock/Getty Images Plus; brazzo/E+; Michael Blann/DigitalVision; Bezvershenko/iStock/Getty Images Plus; Pavel Naumov/iStock/Getty Images Plus; Turgay Malikli/iStock/Getty Images Plus; ONYXprj/iStock/Getty Images Plus; Turgay Malikli/iStock/Getty Images Plus; marina_ua/iStock/Getty Images Plus; **U5**: vkp-australia/iStock Editorial; Pablo Fernandes/iStock Editorial; Dr_Flash/iStock/Getty Images Plus; Vesnaandjic/E+; Peter Adams/Stone; richard eppedio/iStock/Getty Images Plus; George Pachantouris/Moment Unreleased; Maremagnum/Corbis Documentary; choochart choochaikupt/iStock/Getty Images Plus; Dragoncello/iStock/Getty Images Plus; PT Images; Sergii Gnatiuk/iStock/Getty Images Plus; ArtistGNDphotography/E+; aogreatkim/iStock/Getty Images Plus; Westend61; anyaberkut/iStock/Getty Images Plus; da-vooda/iStock/Getty Images Plus; GreenTana/iStock/Getty Images Plus; Library of Congress/Corbis Historical; PytyCzech/iStock/Getty Images Plus; ROBOTOK/iStock/Getty Images Plus; machinim/DigitalVision Vectors; izusek/E+; Peter Muller/Cultura; Sawek Kawila/EyeEm; ljubaphoto/E+; LeoPatrizi/E+; andresr/E+; gbh007/iStock/Getty Images Plus; bubaone/DigitalVision Vectors; yorkfoto/E+; Evgeniya Chertova/iStock/Getty Images Plus; seamartini/iStock/Getty Images Plus; Kisada Muanta/iStock/Getty Images Plus; nadyaillyustrator/iStock/Getty Images Plus; perisuta/iStock/Getty Images Plus; Olga Kurbatova/iStock/Getty Images Plus; Six_Characters/E+; danielvfung/iStock/Getty Images Plus; Fraser Hall/The Image Bank; gionnixxx/iStock Unreleased; George Hammerstein/The Image Bank; Waitforlight/Moment; nukrist/iStock/Getty Images Plus; Sergey Kucherov/Moment; Gonzalo Azumendi/Stone; Nicole Vanessa Agus/EyeEm; CBCK-Christine/iStock/Getty Images Plus; monkeybusinessimages/iStock/Getty Images Plus; **U6**: Tim Macpherson/Stone; pop_jop/DigitalVision Vectors ; Adam Pretty/Getty Images Sport; Mark Kolbe/Getty Images Sport; Karwai Tang/WireImage; Kelly Cestari/World Surf League; Brian Bahr/Getty Images Sport; Alexander Hassenstein/Getty Images Sport; dikobraziy/iStock/Getty Images Plus; Ecelop/iStock/Getty Images Plus; Ewen Charlton/Moment; Victor Habbick Visions/Science Photo Library; MicrovOne/iStock/Getty Images Plus; yuoak/DigitalVision Vectors; Chainarong Prasertthai/iStock/Getty Images Plus; Christophe Simon/AFP; Rimmagraf/iStock/Getty Images Plus; Vasilis Tsikkinis photos/Moment; bubaone/DigitalVision Vectors; Ponomariova_Maria/iStock/Getty Images Plus; Juanmonino/E+; **R3**: Lanski/iStock/Getty Images Plus; Westend61; Bim/iStock/Getty Images Plus; JethuynhCan/Moment; Galina Zhigalova/EyeEm; Ariel Skelley/DigitalVision; martin-dm/E+; eli_asenova/E+; FrankRamspott/DigitalVisionVectors; **U7**: fstop123/E+; mediaphotos/E+; UniversalImagesGroup/Universal Images Group; Fotomay/iStock/Getty Images Plus; Bettmann; mediaphotos/iStock/Getty Images Plus; schmidt-z/E+; The Washington Post; Joseph Niepce/Hulton